TRAVERSE THEATRE

SCOTLAND'S NEW WRITING THEATRE

Traverse Theatre Company

East Coast Chicken Supper

by Martin J Taylor

cast in order of appearance

Fred	Paul Rattray
Stew	Paul Blair
Gibb	Garry Collins
Malone	Malcolm Shields

Director	Richard Wilson
Associate Director	Lorne Campbell
Designer	Fiona Watt
Lighting Designer	Jo Town
Sound Designer	John Harris
Fight Director	Terry King
Voice/Dialect Coach	Ros Steen
Stage Manager	Barry McCall
Deputy Stage Manager	Sunita Hinduja
Assistant Stage Manager	Alison Brodie
Wardrobe Supervisor	Aileen Sherry

**First performed at the Traverse Theatre,
Edinburgh, on Tuesday 2 August 2005**

TRAVERSE THEATRE

Powerhouse of new writing DAILY TELEGRAPH
Artistic Director Philip Howard

The Traverse is Scotland's new writing theatre. Founded in 1963 by a group of maverick artists and enthusiasts, it began as an imaginative attempt to capture the spirit of adventure and experimentation of the Edinburgh Festival all year round. Throughout the decades, the Traverse has evolved and grown in artistic output and ambition. It has refined its mission by strengthening its commitment to producing new plays by Scottish and international playwrights and actively nurturing them throughout their careers. Traverse productions have been seen worldwide and tour regularly throughout the UK and overseas.

The Traverse has produced over 600 new plays in its lifetime and, through a spirit of innovation and risk-taking, has launched the careers of many of the country's best known writers. From, among others, Stanley Eveling in the 1960s, John Byrne in the 1970s, Liz Lochhead in the 1980s, to David Greig and David Harrower in the 1990s, the Traverse is unique in Scotland in its dedication to new writing. It fulfils the crucial role of providing the infrastructure, professional support and expertise to ensure the development of a dynamic theatre culture for Scotland.

The Traverse's activities encompass every aspect of playwriting and pro-duction, providing and facilitating play reading panels, script development workshops, rehearsed readings, public playwriting workshops, writers' groups, discussions and special events. The Traverse's work with young people is of supreme importance and takes the form of encouraging playwriting through its flagship education project Class Act, as well as the Traverse Young Writers' Group. In 2004, the Traverse took the Class Act project to Russia and also staged Articulate, a pilot project with West Dunbartonshire Council for 11 to 14 year olds.

Edinburgh's Traverse Theatre is a mini-festival in itself THE TIMES

From its conception in the 1960s, the Traverse has remained a pivotal venue during the Edinburgh Festival. It receives enormous critical and audience acclaim for its programming, as well as regularly winning awards. In 2001 the Traverse was awarded two Scotsman Fringe Firsts and two Herald Angels for its own productions of Gagarin Way and Wiping My Mother's Arse and a Herald Archangel for overall artistic excellence. In 2002 the Traverse produced award-winning shows, Outlying Islands by David Greig and Iron by Rona Munro and in 2003, The People Next Door by Henry Adam picked up Fringe First and Herald Angel awards before transfering to the Theatre Royal, Stratford East. Re-cast and with a new director, The People Next Door has since toured to Germany, the Balkans and New York. In 2004, the Traverse produced the award-winning Shimmer by Linda McLean and a stage adaptation of Raja Shehadeh's diary account of the Israeli occupation of Ramallah, When The Bulbul Stopped Singing. This play won the Amnesty International Freedom of Expression Award 2004, appeared in January 2005 as part of the Fadjr International Theatre Festival in Tehran and toured to New York in Spring 2005.

To find out about ways to support the Traverse, please contact Norman MacLeod, Development Manager on 0131 228 3223.
www.traverse.co.uk

COMPANY BIOGRAPHIES

Paul Blair (*Stew*) For the Traverse: 15 SECONDS. Other theatre includes: ANNA KARENINA, THE MERCHANT OF VENICE, DR JEKYLL AND MR HYDE (Royal Lyceum, Edinburgh); MACBETH, A LIE OF THE MIND, SCENES FROM AN EXECUTION (Dundee Rep); 8000 M, CASANOVA, LAMENT, CANDIDE 2000 (Suspect Culture); GILT (7:84 tour & Soho); DEALER'S CHOICE, SHINING SOULS, SNOW WHITE, SPEEDRUN, PENETRATOR (Tron Theatre); THE GOOD WOMAN OF SETZUAN, ANTIGONE (TAG Theatre Co); VARIETY (Grid Iron/EIF). Television work includes: TAKIN' OVER THE ASYLUM, STRATHBLAIR, LIFE SUPPORT, RUFFIAN HEARTS (BBC); TAGGART: DEATH TRAP, A FEW BAD MEN, CRACKED (STV); YOU CAN'T BE TOO CAREFUL (ITV/Blue Heaven). Radio Includes: OLALLA, THE LOWLAND CLEARANCES, IN THE ABSENCE OF ANGELS, LOVE AND MONGOOSES, (Radio 4); THE COMMUTER (Radio 3). Film includes: THIS YEAR'S LOVE (Kismet); LEGEND OF THE LOCH (IMAX Prod); HEAVENLY PURSUITS (Island). As co-founder of the production company 'Brocken Spectre', Paul has produced two short films. *The Turning Tide* and *Rank* (BAFTA-nominated Best Short Film 2003).

Lorne Campbell (Associate Director) Trained: Channel 4 Theatre Director's Scheme, RSAMD and Liverpool John Moores. Lorne joined the Traverse in 2002 and since then has been Director on IN THE BAG and THE NEST and Assistant Director on DARK EARTH, OUTLYING ISLANDS, MR PLACEBO, HOMERS and THE SLAB BOYS TRILOGY. Other theatre credits include: THE DUMB WAITER, DEATH AND THE MAIDEN, AN EVENING WITH DAMON RUNYON, A COMEDY OF ERRORS, AS YOU LIKE IT, JOURNEY'S END (Forge Theatre); THE CHAIRS (RSAMD); THE CHEVIOT, THE STAG AND THE BLACK BLACK OIL (Taigh Chearsabhagh).

Garry Collins (*Gibb*) For the Traverse: MR PLACEBO. Other theatre includes: BABY DOLL, A HANDFUL OF DUST, CLEO CAMPING EMMANUELLE & DICK, SNOW WHITE, THE QUEEN OF SPADES, VENICE PRESERVED (Citizens' Theatre); FIERCE, THE HOUGHMAGANDIE PACK, DECKY DOES A BRONCO (Grid Iron); DR KORCZAK'S EXAMPLE (TAG Theatre Co); CAVE DWELLERS (7:84); BEAUTY AND THE BEAST, COMEDY OF ERRORS, CINDERELLA, ROMEO AND JULIET (Royal Lyceum, Edinburgh). Television work includes: THE BOOK GROUP, WITCHCRAZE (BBC2); YOUNG PERSONS GUIDE TO BECOMING A ROCK STAR (Channel 4); LIFE SUPPORT (BBC1). Film includes: DEAR FRANKIE (Scorpio Films).

John Harris (Sound Designer) For the Traverse: THE NEST, FAMILY, KILL THE OLD TORTURE THEIR YOUNG, PERFECT DAYS, GRETA, KNIVES IN HENS, ANNA WEISS, SHARP SHORTS. Other theatre composition includes: SOLSTICE, MIDWINTER (Royal Shakespeare Company); DRUMMERS (Out of Joint); IL BELLISSIMO SILENCIO, STOCKAREE, OF NETTLES AND ROSES (Theatre Workshop). Other composition includes: THE EMPEROR (Channel 4); THE GREEN MAN OF KNOWLEDGE (S4C); and works for the Hebrides Ensemble and Paragon Ensemble. John was artistic director of the Paragon Ensemble 2001 - 2004. He is the founding director of the online contemporary music station Seven Things I Daren't Express, and performs and composes with his own ensemble, Spke.

Terry King (Fight Director): For the Traverse: THE PEOPLE NEXT DOOR, IRON, GAGARIN WAY. For the National Theatre: FOOL FOR LOVE (Peter Gill), KING LEAR (David Hare), OTHELLO (Sam Mendes), HENRY V (Nick Hytner), LONDON CUCKOLDS (Terry Johnson), TING TANG MINE (Michael Rudman), DUCHESS OF MALFI (Phillida Lloyd), JERRY SPRINGER THE OPERA (Stewart Lee), ELMINA'S KITCHEN (Angus Jackson), EDMOND (Edward Hall). For the RSC: TROILUS AND CRESSIDA (Sam Mendes), ROMEO AND JULIET, CYMBELINE (Adrian Noble), PERICLES (David Thacker), TWELFTH NIGHT (Ian Judge), HENRY IV Pts 1 & 2 (Michael Attenbourgh), HENRY VI Pts 1, 2 & 3 (Michael Boyd), MACBETH (Greg Doran), THE JACOBEAN SEASON (Swan), CORIOLANUS (David Farr). For the Royal Court: THE RECRUITING OFFICER (Max Stafford-Clark), SEARCH AND DESTROY (Stephen Daldry), ASHES AND SAND (Ian Rickson), OLEANNA (Harold Pinter), BERLIN BERTIE (Danny Boyle), GREENLAND (Simon Curtis). Other theatre includes: CALIGULA, ACCIDENTAL DEATH OF AN ANARCHIST (Donmar); LYSISTRATA (Old Vic); DEATH OF A SALESMAN (Bristol); OF MICE AND MEN (Nottingham). Opera and musicals include: PORGY AND BESS (Trevor Nunn); OTELLO (Peter Stein); JESUS CHRIST SUPERSTAR (Gael Edwards); SATURDAY NIGHT FEVER (Arlene Philips); CHITTY CHITTY BANG BANG (Adrian Noble).

Paul Rattray (*Fred*) For the Traverse: SHIMMER. Other theatre includes: IN THE BLUE (Theatre 504/Young Vic); COOL WATER MURDER (Belgrade); THE ANATOMIST (Royal Lyceum, Edinburgh); HAND BAG (ATC, Lyric Hammersmith); WOLFSKIN (Hardware); PLAYING THE GAME (Edinburgh Festival); DECKY DOES A BRONCO (Grid Iron); DINNER (National Theatre). Television work includes: CASUALTY (BBC); LAST RIGHTS, SIMPLE THINGS, WET WORK (Channel 4); THE BILL (ITV). Film includes: CREEP (Pathe); MIKE

BASSETT ENGLAND MANAGER (Artists Independent Network/Film Council/Hallmark Entertainment); MORVERN CALLAR (Company Pictures); ENIGMA (Broadway Pictures); MAX (Natural Nylon/Pathe/Film Council); FURNISHED ROOM (Loud Mouse Productions Ltd).

Malcolm Shields (*Malone*) For the Traverse: TRAINSPOTTING (co-production with the Citizens and The Bush). Other theatre includes: SLEEPING BEAUTY, OTHELLO, THE PRINCESS AND THE GOBLIN, JULIUS CAESAR (Royal Lyceum Edinburgh); SCROOGE, THE IMPORTANCE OF BEING EARNEST; OBSERVE THE SONS OF ULSTER MARCHING TOWARD THE SOMME, A MIDSUMMER NIGHT'S DREAM (Citizens Theatre); YOU'LL HAVE HAD YOUR HOLE (West Yorkshire Playhouse); THE RED BALLOON (National Theatre); JOCK TAMSIN'S BAIRNS, CYRANO (Communicado). Television work includes: THE BELLROCK, CASUALTY, THE LOST WORLD, MONARCH OF THE GLEN, LOOKING AFTER JO JO, BAD BOYS (BBC); INSPECTOR REBUS: DEAD SOULS, INSPECTOR REBUS: BLACK & BLUE (STV); IN DEFENCE (ITV); HOUND OF THE BASKERVILLES (Tiger Aspect). Film includes: PORK CHOP (Cineworks); YOUNG ADAM (Film Council/Hanway Films); GIRL IN THE LAY-BY (APT Films); POACHED (Freshwater Films). Radio includes: HENRY V (BBC/Open University). Malcolm also works as a movement director for stage and screen.

Ros Steen (Voice/Dialect Coach): Trained: RSAMD. Has worked extensively in theatre, film and TV. For the Traverse: IN THE BAG, THE SLAB BOYS TRILOGY, DARK EARTH, HOMERS, OUTLYING ISLANDS, THE BALLAD OF CRAZY PAOLA, THE TRESTLE AT POPE LICK CREEK, HERITAGE (2001 and 1998), AMONG UNBROKEN HEARTS, SHETLAND SAGA, SOLEMN MASS FOR A FULL MOON IN SUMMER (as co-director), KING OF THE FIELDS, HIGHLAND SHORTS, FAMILY, KILL THE OLD TORTURE THEIR YOUNG, THE CHIC NERDS, GRETA, LAZYBED, KNIVES IN HENS, PASSING PLACES, BONDAGERS, ROAD TO NIRVANA, SHARP SHORTS, MARISOL, GRACE IN AMERICA. Other theatre credits includes: TWELFTH NIGHT, DANCING AT LUGHNASA, DUCHESS OF MALFI, (Dundee Rep); BASH, DAMN JACOBITE BITCHES, OBSERVE THE SONS OF ULSTER MARCHING TOWARDS THE SOMME (Citizens' Theatre); WORD FOR WORD (Magnetic North); CAVE DWELLERS (7:84); EXILES (Jerwood Young Directors/Young Vic); THE PRIME OF MISS JEAN BRODIE, PLAYBOY OF THE WESTERN WORLD (Royal Lyceum, Edinburgh). Film credits include: THE ADVENTURES OF GREYFRIARS BOBBY (Piccadilly Pictures); GREGORY'S TWO GIRLS (Channel Four Films). Television credits include: SEA OF SOULS, ROCKFACE, 2000 ACRES OF SKY (BBC).

Martin J Taylor (Writer) Born in Kirkcaldy in 1971, Martin trained on the Theatre Art course in Kirkcaldy in 1990 and at the Drama Centre, London in 1999. EAST COAST CHICKEN SUPPER is his first play to receive a full production. He is currently working on short film scripts and a new full-length play.

Fiona Watt (Designer) For the Traverse: DARK EARTH, OUTLYING ISLANDS (also Jerwood Theatre Upstairs and World Stages Festival, Toronto), THE TRESTLE AT POPE LICK CREEK, HERITAGE, HIGHLAND SHORTS. Other theatre includes: OTHELLO (Nottingham Playhouse); THE BEAUTY QUEEN OF LEENANE, BOSTON MARRIAGE (Bolton Octagon); THE WEIR (Lyric Theatre, Belfast); DEALER'S CHOICE (The Tron); OUTWARD BOUND (Palace Theatre, Watford). Opera credits include: GOOD ANGEL, BAD ANGEL (Hebrides Ensemble), LA PIETRA DEL PARAGONE, MAVRA, RIDERS TO THE SEA, GIANNI SCHICCHI (RSAMD). Fiona has exhibited her work at TIME + SPACE (CCA) and 2D>3D (Sheffield Millennium Galleries & UK tour).

Richard Wilson (Director) An award-winning actor and one of the foremost directors of new writing in the UK, Richard is currently the visiting professor for Drama at Glasgow University and Associate Director of the Royal Court Theatre. His recent directorial credits include: THE WOMAN BEFORE, PLAYING THE VICTIM (co-production with Told by an Idiot); UNDER THE WHALEBACK, A DAY IN THE DULL ARMOUR / GRAFITTI, WHERE DO WE LIVE, I JUST STOPPED BY TO SEE THE MAN (Royal Court Theatre, London); PRIMO (National Theatre/The Music Box Theatre, Broadway). His most recent and enduring TV credits include: DR WHO, BORN AND BRED and ONE FOOT IN THE GRAVE (BBC). Film credits include: WOMEN TALKING DIRTY (Rocket Pictures); SOFT TOP HARD SHOULDER (Gruber Bros); HOW TO GET AHEAD IN ADVERTISING (Handmade Films); PRICK UP YOUR EARS (BFI); PASSAGE TO INDIA (Zenith).

For their help on EAST COAST CHICKEN SUPPER the Traverse thanks

RSAMD, Dundee Rep, Peter Rankin.

For their support, inspiration and occasional lodgings Martin J Taylor would like to thank

Andy T & Will H, George T, Ian Gibson, James Halliday, Kemi, Kurt, Lara D, Maley, Mel & Paul, Peter McLaughlin, Paul Rattray, Ron, Sam Penn and Derek, The Southwark RTB Girls, Tom and Shelley, Phillip Howard, Richard Wilson and Joe Totale NWRA.

SPONSORSHIP

Sponsorship income enables the Traverse to commission
and produce new plays and to offer audiences a diverse and
exciting programme of events throughout the year. We would like
to thank the following companies for their support:

CORPORATE SPONSORS

ANNIVERSARY ANGELS

Whiteburn
projects limited

BAILLIE GIFFORD

BENNETT & ROBERTSON LLP

grey friars
chartered accountants

New Horizons
Computer Learning Centers
Scotland

edNET
internetworkingsolutions

People & Projects

With thanks to

Claire Aitken of Royal Bank of Scotland for mentoring support arranged through the Arts & Business Mentoring Scheme. Purchase of the Traverse Box Office, computer network and technical and training equipment has been made possible with money from The Scottish Arts Council National Lottery Fund

Scottish
Arts Council
LOTTERY FUNDED

The Traverse Theatre's work
would not be possible without the support of

Scottish
Arts Council

·EDINBVRGH·
THE CITY OF EDINBURGH COUNCIL

The Traverse Theatre receives financial assistance from

The Calouste Gulbenkian Foundation, The Peggy Ramsay
Foundation, The Binks Trust, The Bulldog Prinsep Theatrical Fund,
The Esmée Fairbairn Foundation, The Gordon Fraser Charitable
Trust, The Garfield Weston Foundation, The Paul Hamlyn
Foundation, The Craignish Trust, Lindsay's Charitable Trust,
The Tay Charitable Trust, The Ernest Cook Trust, The Wellcome
Trust, The Sir John Fisher Foundation, The Ruben and Elisabeth
Rausing Trust, The Equity Trust Fund, The Cross Trust, N Smith
Charitable Settlement, Douglas Heath Eves Charitable Trust,
The Bill and Margaret Nicol Charitable Trust, The Emile Littler
Foundation, Mrs M Guido's Charitable Trust, Gouvernement du
Québec, The Canadian High Commission, The British Council,
The Daiwa Foundation, The Sasakawa Foundation,
The Japan Foundation

Charity No. SC002368

**Sets, props and costumes for
IN THE BAG**
created by Traverse Workshops
(funded by the National Lottery)

Scottish
Arts Council
LOTTERY FUNDED

Production photography by Richard Campbell
Print photography by Euan Myles

**For their continued generous support
of Traverse productions the Traverse thanks**

Habitat, Marks and Spencer, Princes Street
Camerabase, BHS, and Holmes Place

TRAVERSE THEATRE – THE COMPANY

EAST COAST CHICKEN SUPPER

Martin J Taylor

For Sandra Dixon

Characters

GIBB, *mid-twenties*

FRED, *mid-twenties*

STEW, *two years older than Fred and Gibb*

MALONE, *late thirties. The local radge*

The action takes place in a small Fife coastal town.

Scene One

Living room/kitchen area of a cottage. Downstage left, a door leading to the back garden. Upstage right, a door leading to the hallway, and the front door. A music system including turntable, amp, speakers, tape deck, CD player. CD rack and a decent stack of vinyl. A sofa, armchair, coffee table stage right. Kitchen table and chairs stage left. FRED and STEW standing, GIBB seated in the middle of the sofa, still wearing his jacket.

FRED. He doesnae get it.

STEW. Okay. Now this is it. One minute you're here. And the next . . . you're gone. Boom, vanished. Not a word not a trace.

FRED. Total fuckin mystery.

STEW. And then what? Ay? People start to notice, people talk, they want to know, so what do they do? They ask us.

FRED. Everybody's asking us.

STEW. Cos obviously they assume we should know. Because guess what, ay, we're you're friends.

FRED. We are your friends. Aren't we?

STEW. Course we're his friends.

FRED. We are still friends ay Gibby?

STEW. Fuck sake Fred, why d'you think he came here?

FRED. Where else was he gonna go?

Pause.

STEW. So anyway you fuck off for no apparent reason and you leave me and Fred here to deal with the consequences. Namely half the scumbags in the town bombarding us with questions.

FRED. Like where's he gone, why's he gone, when's he coming back . . .

STEW. Yea, questions we don't know the answers to.

FRED. Which to be honest kinda sucks.

STEW. See now this increased level of interest in our business may well be unwanted, but in the beginning . . .

FRED. It's understandable.

STEW. It's totally understandable. Don't get me wrong it's a pain in the arse but, yea I can see where they're coming from.

FRED. Initially.

STEW. That's what I'm sayin, up to a point. Up to a point it's perfectly acceptable behaviour, under the circumstances.

FRED. I'd do the same.

STEW. Course you would. We all would. But, Christ man this goes on for a while. And you can call me naïve but I wasnae expecting it.

FRED. Naw me neither.

STEW. It's a small town Gibb, word gets around fast.

FRED. Aye, but guess what?

STEW. What?

FRED. Curiosity lingers.

STEW. Damn fuckin right it lingers.

FRED. The point is Gibby everybody knew you'd gone, but we had nothing to tell them.

STEW. Naw we never knew fuck-all did we?

FRED. Not a fuckin scoobie.

STEW. But what, d'you think that stops them?

FRED. Like fuck it does.

STEW. You got to remember Gibby, this isnae our town man.

FRED. Naw there's no friends here.

Pause.

STEW. How long d'you think it took Gibby, you know, before people were actually resigned to the fact that we had absolutely sweet fuck-all to offer them in the way of an explanation?

GIBB. I dunno.

STEW. What do you think.

GIBB. I dunno how long?

STEW. Too fuckin long.

FRED. Actually it was about three or four months.

4

STEW. Three or four months Gibby.

FRED. Oh aye at least three or four months.

STEW. See . . . in a wee town that's a long time Gibby. A town this size it's a fuckin age.

FRED. And it's never really gone away has it Stew?

STEW. Naw I cannae say it fuckin has.

FRED. In fact you could say that was just the start of it.

Pause.

STEW. All we ever tried to do since we came here Gibby was to go about our business, keep our fuckin heads down . . .

FRED. And stay out of trouble.

STEW. Tell him what it was like.

FRED. What it was like?

STEW. I want him to know.

FRED. What it was like?

STEW. Aye.

FRED. The initial onslaught?

STEW. Aye.

FRED. The incessant fuckin pestering when we walked down the street?

STEW. All that shite.

FRED. The rare occasions we went to the boozer?

STEW. I'm talking about the little sideways glances.

FRED. The wind-ups. The childish sniggers, the endless stream of provocation?

STEW. All of it.

FRED. Oh Jesus man, where d'you start? You've no idea Gibby. The same bunch of lowlifes coming out with the same old shite every time we ran into them.

STEW. You've no idea Gibby, I'm telling you man you've no fuckin idea.

FRED. And you really want me to tell him what it was like?

STEW. Damn right I do.

FRED. Fair enough.

STEW. I want him to know.

Pause.

FRED. Well mate, what can I say . . . It wasnae nice was it?

STEW. No it wasnae nice.

FRED. Fuck no, you couldnae say it was pleasant could you?

STEW. Naw an this is us just giving you the edited highlights.

FRED. Yea, we choose to spare you Gibby we really do.

STEW. Aye cos we're all best neebours here like.

FRED. Naw we wouldnae want you to think we were putting you on a guilt trip or nothing, I mean you're just in the door but in reality, it was actually –

STEW. It was a damn sight worse.

FRED. It was a fuck of a lot worse.

STEW. Shit man, think about it, for a second Gibby, I mean what were we supposed to say? Ay? We don't know? We never saw? He never told us nothing?

FRED. Think about it.

STEW. The fact is the guy's gone end of story, all right. That's all we know, that's all we can say, so just . . . just leave us the fuck alone why don't you.

Pause.

FRED. *We* never said leave us alone did we?

STEW. No I know *we* never said leave us alone.

FRED. Did you say leave us alone?

STEW. Course I fuckin never said leave –

FRED. All right man, I'm just asking.

STEW. I know, and I'm just saying.

FRED. Good . . . cos . . . well you know it's a bit . . .

STEW. What?

FRED. It's a bit fuckin gay likes.

STEW. Ay?

FRED. I said it's a bit fuckin gay.

STEW. Aye I know that's what you said but –

FRED. I'm just saying, you know, saying leave us alone, to say leave us alone to these kinds of people sounds just a wee bit on the gay side.

STEW. Which is why I never said it.

FRED. You never?

STEW. Course I fuckin never . . . I might have wanted to . . .

FRED. But you didn't.

STEW. Exactly.

FRED. Cos you knew what folk would think.

STEW. Course I know what folk'll think, all I'm saying is that inside . . .

FRED. It's what you were thinking.

STEW. Correct.

FRED. Leave me alone. Get out of my fucking space.

STEW. Yea.

FRED. That's how you felt?

STEW. Yea, you know, in my guts.

FRED. Get the fuck out of here.

STEW. Yea.

FRED. Piss off.

STEW. Aye.

FRED. Just go away or I'll get ma sister ontae you.

STEW. Ay?

FRED. Nothing just . . .

STEW. What?

FRED. What?

STEW. What the fuck you trying to say Fred? (*Takes two Valium.*)

FRED. Me? Nothing. No, I wasnae saying fuck-all like. I was just having a . . . you know just trying to . . . Christ you're touchy the day Stew. An by the way, what have I told you about that?

STEW. What?

FRED. I've told you, no pharmaceuticals during office hours.

STEW. It helps me to relax.

FRED. It clouds your judgement is what it does.

STEW. What are you ma maw or something?

FRED*'s mobile beeps as he receives a text message.*

Who is it?

FRED. It's Cheesy.

STEW. What the fuck does he want?

FRED. Here.

STEW. Tell him we're busy.

FRED. You tell him.

STEW. It's your mobile.

FRED. He's your fuckin neebour.

STEW. He's no ma fuckin neebour all right.

FRED. Whatever he's your guy. You mind Cheesy don't you Gibby?

GIBB. I dunno, I think so.

FRED. He remembers you.

GIBB. Aye? He's the wee freckly guy with the ginger hair?

FRED. Stew's well in with him.

STEW. I sort him out. That's as far as it goes.

FRED. The guy's a fuckin fanny.

STEW. I know what he is.

FRED. Anyway he wants you to give him a call.

STEW. Fuck it. Text the guy and tell him we'll call him back.

FRED. We?

STEW. Tell him I'll call him back.

FRED. When?

STEW. Later.

FRED. When later?

STEW. I dunno, before five. Can you do that for me?

FRED. Aye I think I can manage.

STEW. Good. Anyway . . . You want a fag Gibb?

GIBB. No thanks mate.

STEW. No?

GIBB. I've given up.

STEW. You're kidding?

GIBB. Aye man.

STEW. So have a fuckin fag man.

GIBB. Naw man. I've given up.

STEW. When was this likes?

GIBB. When I was in London.

STEW. Did I say where? Fred.

FRED. What?

STEW. Did I say where?

FRED. I dunno, I wasnae paying attention.

STEW. Naw well I never, I said when, how long, how long have you been a non-smoker, that's what I was –

GIBB. About a couple of months.

STEW. No fuckin way.

GIBB. Aye it's been about a couple of months as I recall.

STEW. Good for you mate.

GIBB. I mean I don't know the exact date, I never made a note or nothin.

STEW. I cannae get enough of them myself likes. So you must be over the worst then?

GIBB. Aye I seem to be.

STEW. An you never get no cravings?

GIBB. Nah, no really.

STEW. Never?

GIBB. Nothin major.

STEW. What about when you're drinking?

GIBB. It's hard at first, but I wanted to stop so I stopped.

STEW. Fair play to you mate.

GIBB. Well you know . . . a bit of will power that's all.

STEW. Naw I mean it, well done.

GIBB. Hey it's not fuckin rocket science is it?

STEW. Nah, I don't suppose it is. (*Pause. To* FRED.) I wonder why he never called me?

FRED. I dunno maybe he did.

STEW. You seen ma mobile?

FRED. Not recently.

STEW. Shite.

FRED. Have you tried your jacket pocket?

STEW. I havenae tried anywhere yet.

FRED. All right well try your jacket pocket.

STEW. Aye good idea. (*Pause.*) Have you seen my jacket?

FRED. Which one?

STEW. The one I was wearing last night.

FRED. The blue one?

STEW. Aye.

FRED. It's upstairs.

STEW. Whereabouts upstairs?

FRED. Hanging over the banister.

STEW. I'll go an get it then.

   STEW *exits.*

FRED. I swear to God I'm like his fuckin maw these days.

GIBB. Is he all right?

FRED. Stew?

GIBB. He seems a bit . . .

FRED. What?

GIBB. I dunno.

FRED. Confused?

GIBB. Edgy.

FRED. He needs to lay off the fuckin chems. They're fuckin with his head. Anyway . . . aye, me and Stew are constantly getting all this shite fired at us which to be honest got to be a right pain in the starfish. So eventually the standard response became . . . ask his mum . . . Why don't you ask his mum cos we don't know fuck-all. Course if we did it would have been a different story, it wouldnae've been as bad.

STEW *enters.*

Would it Stew? Would it?

STEW. Ma battery's flat.

FRED. Aye? Yea, so, they keep at it, you know . . . they're saying aye but you guys are his mates, you guys ken him. An we're sayin, yea we know him, but it's not exactly like we follow him to the bogs so why don't you go ask his mum? Well where the fuck is she? I mean it's just a game to them, they've no intention of going anywhere so we say, ay, she's forty miles up the road in Tayport and guess what, we dinnae have the address, which seems to put them off, cos every time we told whoever it was who was asking, and we had them all didn't we Stew?

STEW. Oh aye.

FRED. I mean who did we get?

STEW. Well Cheesy and Malone for starters.

GIBB. Who the fuck is Malone?

FRED. Aw nobody special.

GIBB. I don't remember him.

STEW. Naw you wouldnae.

GIBB. So who is he?

STEW. Nobody special.

FRED. Nah he's just your ordinary bog-standard run-of-the-mill psychopath. Every town's got one . . . this town's got him.

GIBB. I cannae mind hearing about him.

FRED. Naw well you wouldnae cos he just got out of jail.

GIBB. Aw right, what for?

FRED. For raping his own wife whilst she was still pregnant and threatening to strangle her wee boy.

STEW. Who wasnae his.

GIBB. Nice.

FRED. Oh aye he's a right fuckin charmer. Who else was there?

STEW. I dunno . . . Beano . . . Mikey Syme and all his crowd.

FRED. Squeak, Spenny . . .

STEW. Spook . . . Tommy T . . .

FRED. Beak Hal . . .

STEW. Plus the rest.

FRED. Aye all the usual suspects and practically to a man when we said she's forty miles up the road they all said, or words to the effect . . . Oh but we're not gonna drive all the way up to Tayport. Aye, fuck that for a game of soldiers, we wouldnae do it even if we had the address. So we're like, oh but pardon me, but a minute ago you seemed awfy keen. And they say, oh aye we are keen but . . . and they leave it hanging in the air. Which means what? I mean what the fuck does that mean ay?

STEW. It means they're a bunch of fuckin low-life cunts. A bunch of dirty fuckin vultures.

FRED. That's about the size of it.

STEW. I mean, what, d'you think they care Gibby? Do you? Bollocks man. No, we care. Your friends, us, the ones you left behind.

FRED. I hope you're starting to build a picture.

STEW. But . . . did we put you down? Did we cut you off? Cos we could have. We could have said anything, you know. We could have shrugged our shoulders, rubbed your nose in the dirt an dragged your name right through the mud. And what . . . in the long run d'you think that would have done us any harm?

FRED. To distance ourselves from you.

STEW. I mean d'you think it would have been any skin off our backs to just totally disown you?

FRED. Cos that was always an option Gibby.

STEW. In fact our standing in the town might have risen if we'd have adopted that kind of approach don't you think?

FRED. Hey feel free to speak out any time you want Gibb.

Pause.

STEW. But naw man, we stayed loyal.

FRED. We covered up.

STEW. We kept it tight man, kept it fuckin close. No there was no name-calling and back-biting coming from this direction.

FRED. At least not in public anyway.

STEW. Even though, if you want to know the truth, we were left looking like a couple of fucking clowns.

FRED. On more than one occasion.

STEW. I felt like a fuckin clown.

FRED. Which is no fun at all.

STEW. I'm telling you Gibby, I havenae felt so stupid since I got my finger stuck up my nose with Super Glue and that was fucking ages ago.

FRED. Primary Two.

STEW. Naw naw I think you'll find it was Primary Four Fred.

FRED. Was it?

STEW. Aye.

FRED. You sure about that?

STEW. Course I'm fuckin sure. It was summer term, Primary Four.

FRED. Aye?

STEW. Aye. It was Miss Fox's class. An I know it was summer term cos I had chronic hay fever. I had snot dribbling down my hand, down my elbow and making this wee pool on my desk. I never had nae tissues or nothing. Miss Fox thought she'd make an example of me in front of the rest of the class before she sent me to the school doctor. Shit like that you never forget. It stays with you.

FRED. Hey man, I wasnae disputing the finer points of what was obviously a defining moment in your childhood all I was saying was it was Primary Two.

STEW. It was Primary Four.

FRED. Aye, you sure about that?

STEW. I'm fuckin positive. You were in Primary Two, I was in Primary Four.

FRED. Oh aye.

STEW. Exactly.

FRED. Right enough. But I was half-right though.

STEW. Naw man you were all wrong.

FRED. Naw naw, hold on a sec. When was it you got your finger stuck up your nose? I was in Primary Two and you were in Primary Four, mate, I hate to tell you but that's the same point in time, it's just a slightly different way of looking at it. (*To* GIBB.) Is it not?

GIBB. I dunno, more or less I suppose.

FRED. See.

STEW. Look this is all completely by-the-fuckin-by. We're straying from the –

GIBB. What were you doing with Super Glue in the first place?

STEW. I don't know do I? The point is they were laughing at us. Weren't they Fred?

FRED. What? Oh aye, everybody, the whole fuckin town.

STEW. In the pub. On the street. Probably even in the post office when we're cashing our Giros. But we stood by you.

FRED. Even when the rumours started.

GIBB. What rumours?

STEW. Cos, when all's said and done Gibby, you're our mate.

GIBB. What's all this about rumours?

STEW. Fuck the rumours. (*Pause.*) You hurt ma feelings Gibby, an I know that sounds a bit –

FRED. Sounds a bit fuckin homosexual to me like.

STEW. I'm trying to tell him something.

FRED. I'm just trying to lighten the fuckin mood a bit. There's no need to be so . . . so fuckin sensitive . . . it's hard work man.

Pause.

STEW. Look you know me Gibb, I'm a gentle man, but I have to tell you I had a lot of bad feelings towards you, I'm talking violent thoughts. Oh yea, I thought long and hard about what I was going to do to you if I ever saw you again. Am I being too strong?

FRED. What after all the abuse we've taken?

STEW. That's what I'm getting at.

FRED. There's no such thing in my book.

STEW. Fuckin right there isnae. (*Pause.*) So anyway, what're you saying to it Tone?

GIBB. What do you mean?

STEW. I mean what are you sayin to it?

GIBB. Fuck it, I dunno, what can I say?

STEW. How the fuck should I know Tone, that's why I'm asking you.

GIBB. Look guys, I realise it's probably not much consolation, but for what it's worth . . . I had my reasons.

FRED. For going?

GIBB. Yea.

STEW. And?

GIBB (*goes to the fridge*). And nothing, I just –

STEW. You had your reasons.

GIBB. Yea you know.

STEW. And that's the best you can do? A fuckin year and that's all we get.

GIBB. Come on guys ay, what am I meant to say? (*Inspects the fridge.*) Anyone want anything?

STEW. No no, you just make yourself at home pal.

GIBB. Fred?

FRED. Eh . . . aye get us a can of Red Stripe Gibby. Cold ones are at the back.

GIBB. Stew.

STEW. What?

GIBB. You want a tin?

STEW. No thanks mate, you just look after yourself.

GIBB (*takes a can of Red Stripe and fixes himself a glass of milk*). You want a glass Fred?

FRED. Nah just gimme the tin. Good man.

GIBB. Cheers.

FRED. Cheers.

Pause.

STEW. What can I say Gibb? It's a fuckin slap in the face.

FRED. Christ you cannae whack a cold can of Red Stripe can you? Cheers Gibby.

STEW. I mean you know me Tone, I'm an emotional guy, I try to hide it but this is . . . this is fuckin . . .

FRED. Serious?

STEW. It's well fuckin serious.

GIBB. All right, point taken. D'you want me to explain?

STEW. Well I dunno, I mean I wouldn't want to put you out like.

FRED. Aye dinnae go out your way for us Gibb.

STEW. Yea cos so far, what you've said since you walked in that door.

FRED. And you havenae said much.

STEW. Naw exactly, he hasn't said much at all, that's my point. We . . . I, expected more. See the first time a guy opens his mouth that's the most important time, when it's still hanging in the balance, it can go one way or the other, like two sides of the same coin.

GIBB. I'm not quite getting what you're trying to –

STEW. The point is I'm the injured party and I'm no gonna make it easy for you. It's up to you to bust your fuckin guts to convince us, even if you cannae get a word in edgeways I want to see you popping veins cos if it was me that was in your shoes I'd be breaking my fuckin back to make amends.

GIBB. Fuck me, you guys . . . you guys are really taking this . . .

STEW. The word is serious. And yes Anthony we fuckin are.

FRED. You can see why can't you?

STEW. Well. (*Pause.*) It's a one-word answer Gibb.

FRED. Yes or no?

STEW. It's that simple.

FRED. Make a choice.

STEW. C'mon man take a fuckin stand.

FRED. To ease our pain.

STEW. Yes or no?

FRED. Help us out.

STEW. It's not fuckin rocket science man. One fuckin word is all I'm asking.

FRED. Yes or no.

GIBB. Yes.

STEW. Yes?

GIBB. Yes.

STEW. And . . . ?

GIBB. You asked for one word, I gave you one word.

STEW. Just yes?

GIBB. Yea man.

STEW. Yea man what?

GIBB. I dunno. Yes sir, I'm sorry. What . . . I dunno, I'm sorry I've been a bad boy an I've misbehaved an I promise I'll never do it again. How's that?

STEW. Ay? What the fuck's all that about?

FRED. Aye you've lost me an all mate.

STEW. You don't need to call me sir . . . Tony, none of this warrants sarcasm . . . What the fuck's all that about?

FRED. You have to answer the question Gibby.

GIBB. Which one?

STEW. What d'you mean which one?

GIBB. I mean this one or the last one?

STEW. The last one.

GIBB. Which was?

STEW. Tell him Fred.

FRED. Fuck I dunno.

STEW. Well it was you that asked him it.

FRED. The question was . . . I dunno, Gibby . . .

GIBB. What is it Fred?

FRED. The question, the last question . . .

GIBB. Aw right, you want to know the . . . ?

FRED. Yea, that last one, what was it?

STEW. Why the fuck you asking him?

FRED. Cos I think he knows. Gibby.

GIBB. The question was – can't you see why?

STEW. Why what? Fred?

FRED. I don't fuckin know all right.

STEW (*to* GIBB). Why what?

GIBB. Hey it's you guys doing the asking no me.

STEW. Bunch of fuckin bastards. I mean it I was fuckin close, you know that, I swear to God I was nearly fuckin there.

FRED. Come on Gibby, play the fuckin white man.

STEW. You know how hard it is to actually make a point these days?

FRED. Oh no, it's never easy ay.

STEW. It's like pullin teeth man. I dunno why the fuck I even bother.

Pause.

FRED. Stew.

STEW. What?

FRED. Come on man, what's the matter with you?

STEW. Nothing, I'm fine.

FRED. Gibby. Does Stew look all right to you?

GIBB. Hey Stew, come on mate. Don't give up on us. Me and Fred both want to hear what you have to say. Don't we Fred?

FRED. Absa-fuckin-lutely.

GIBB. Go for it mate. Say what's on your mind.

Pause.

STEW. Okay. Now go with me here. This is just off the top of my head but it's how I'm seeing it right now. (*Pause.*) You know who Garry Kasparov is?

FRED. I dunno is he like an astronaut or something?

STEW. You've never heard of –

FRED. Naw man, he could be spoon bender for all I know.

STEW. Gibby, don't tell me you –

GIBB. Course I know who he is, he's arguably the greatest chess player who ever lived.

STEW. The greatest chess player who –

GIBB. Arguably the greatest chess player.

STEW. Now this Kasparov guy, he's a bona fide genius. And in the course of a game he might take as long as half an hour to make a move, right. To move a piece of wood or ivory a few fuckin inches, from this square to that square. Half an hour just to sacrifice a pawn say, an this guy's a genius.

FRED. A bona fide genius.

STEW. Yea, and not only that but he's got a team of well-paid individuals who research old games from way way back. Who compile this enormous database of moves and games and variations. So that he has questions that no fucker's ever asked and answers to which no other player would ever find a question for. Does that make sense?

FRED. Fuck me Stew, I never knew you had it in you.

STEW. Yea well me, I don't have this luxury. It's just me in here, my memory, with it's fuck-ups, it's foibles and it's failings. D'you get me?

GIBB. Course I do.

STEW. And sometimes in the heat of battle, in the heat of the moment, when I'm trying so hard to forge ahead with my line of reasoning I forget, you know . . . when I'm trying to get to the heart of the matter an I forget where it was I was and how I got to this precise point.

GIBB. I know what you're saying Stew. It's normal.

STEW. And maybe the reason I forget is that, I dunno maybe I care too much. I wish I didn't. I wish I didn't but I do.

GIBB. There's nothing wrong with that.

STEW. Yea well I'd like to think so. So, please I just want you to tell me, please . . . what was the question?

GIBB. The question was, as I remember, literally, can't you see why? Which taken out of context is a tad ambiguous but look, I'm not here to pick you up on –

FRED. Hey Gibb, come on. Now is not the time to score points.

GIBB. Okay, I was being a bit of a prick there. What you were asking was can I see why you guys are taking it so seriously.

STEW. And can you?

GIBB. Well yea sure but you know you could be more specific about what it actually is, you know this 'it' that you keep talking about.

STEW. Okay now I need a drink. Jesus this is such a fuckin toil. You know if somebody had told me when I was young . . .

FRED. Come on Stew you're nearly there.

STEW. Aye no thanks to you.

FRED. Hey man I'm only human.

STEW. You make it so fuckin hard for me Gibby you know that?

GIBB. I don't mean to.

STEW. You make me feel like I'm the one who should be apologising which definitely cannae be right.

FRED. Play the fuckin game Gibby man, we're all friends here.

STEW. Listen. You go away, say nothing. You come back, you say nothing.

FRED. Like two bookends.

STEW. But what about the time in between? For us? To have to put up with . . .

FRED. The ignominy, it means disgrace, you know, I heard Alex Ferguson use it one time and I just –

STEW. Ay?

FRED. I always wanted to get it in. (*Pause.*) I know, it's a big word but I do think it's appropriate.

STEW. Fred . . . For once man. Can you no just shut the fuck up and stop trying to be so fuckin clever all the time. (*Pause. To* GIBB.) All the shite we went through, all the bullshit Gibby. I mean these are dangerous times for us. You can understand why we're pissed off.

GIBB. Course I can.

STEW. You do?

GIBB. Yea . . . yea of course I do. I'm sorry.

STEW. For leaving?

GIBB. Yea.

STEW. For putting us through the mincer?

GIBB. For everything. It was wrong, I was selfish and I apologise. To both of you.

STEW. We were hurt Gibby. You hurt me.

GIBB. I dunno I just got caught up . . .

STEW. You knock at the door, appear out of the blue like it's nothing. And it's not nothing. Nothing is nothing, everything is something. This is something. You're back. Things have been said. We have to talk. Things have changed. Where's ma . . . I need a fuckin Valium. I had a bottle somewhere. (*Looks in the cupboards and drawers.*) You seen my Vallies Fred?

FRED. What the new ones?

STEW. Aye, you seen them?

FRED. Naw.

STEW. Bastard.

FRED. Skin up man, smoke a joint.

STEW. I don't want a fuckin joint. I want ma Vallies. This is fuckin bullshit. There was half a fuckin bottle left in them.

FRED. Don't take any of this to heart Gibby, it's just . . . well I for one am in a wee bit of shock at you coming here unannounced and look at Stew, well he's definitely flustered. I mean what if you'd have croaked?

STEW (*finds an empty bottle of Valium*). I need to go back to the flat. Have you thought about where you're gonna stay?

GIBB. I thought I'd just move back into my old room if that's all right.

STEW. Aye that's fine by me.

GIBB. I mean I wouldnae want to put youse out like.

STEW. Well I've no objections.

GIBB. Cheers man, I appreciate it.

FRED. Hey hold on a minute, time out. Do I no get a vote here? (*Pause.*) We cannae let him get out of this scot-free can we?

STEW. Dinnae be a cunt Fred.

FRED. I'm not. I just don't know if I'm happy with that being the arrangement.

STEW. He's winding you up Gibby.

FRED. What about all the grief?

STEW. Dinnae listen to him.

FRED. And the constant paranoia?

STEW. Who's paranoid like?

FRED. Aw come on man, you get it worse than me.

STEW. Get what?

FRED. The fear, an I know you know what I'm talking about.

GIBB. Guys if it's gonna be a problem –

FRED. And not only that but it's a matter of pride.

GIBB. Look I'll go if it's –

STEW. You're going nowhere.

FRED. Look all I'm saying is there should be a wee bit retribution.

STEW. You're talking out your arse.

FRED. Hear me out. Look we've been going on about how the natives have been tuggin our wires about Gibby fuckin off, an all that other shite. And we can talk all night about the grief and the discomfort, but it means fuck-all compared to the fact that they all know what our line of business is. And like you say we've kept out heads down and tried to do our own thing and we've just about been tolerated. Just. Am I wrong? Am I wrong Stew? But if we'd stepped over the line and got all these inbred fuckers telt, told them it was our fuckin business and no one else's then what? I'll tell you what, we'd either be sitting here minus a limb each or we'd be what, I dunno perish the thought but . . .

STEW. What?

FRED. I reckon we'd probably be . . .

STEW. What?

FRED. Sharing a cell in Saughton.

GIBB. I hear the food at Saughton's no bad.

FRED. I mean any prison which is something I swore was never gonna happen to me.

STEW. Look, he's fuckin staying and that's the end of it.

FRED. He's put us in a compromising situation.

STEW. He's your best mate for fuck sake. Hey Gibby dinnae you be takin his word as –

FRED. It's a matter of pride Stew. You understand Gibb? It's just a matter –

STEW. Are you saying you want to turn him away?

FRED. Listen I know I might not look it but I'm actually a man of high principles.

GIBB. Guys, I don't want to cause any trouble.

STEW. Take your fuckin jacket off. (*To* FRED.) You want to send our oldest friend in the whole world back out onto the streets with no place to go. Is that what you're saying?

FRED. Naw . . . but I had you going though, ay?

STEW. No joke mate but you are without a doubt the biggest fuckin cunt that I have ever met in my entire life.

FRED. Hey I do my best.

Pause.

GIBB. I'll take my stuff upstairs then.

STEW. Come here man. (*Gives* GIBB *a hug.*) I missed you man, I really missed you.

FRED. Aw, see now that's more like it.

STEW. I'm glad you're back.

GIBB. It's good to be back.

STEW. Aye it's all gonna be fuckin nectar man.

GIBB. I know. I'm just gonna dump ma stuff, maybe have a wee wash if that's all right.

STEW. Have a shower if you want.

GIBB. Thanks Stew. And thanks as well Fred.

FRED. No worries . . . it's good to have you back in one piece.

GIBB *exits. Pause.*

STEW. What was all that about?

FRED. What?

STEW. Not letting him stay.

FRED. I was just having a laugh.

STEW. A fuckin laugh.

FRED. What's wrong with that?

STEW. It wasnae funny.

FRED. I got a kick out of it.

STEW. He's just back, we should be . . .

FRED. What?

STEW. I dunno we need to be more . . .

FRED. Well if you dinnae you cannae expect me to.

STEW. We need to make the guy feel welcome.

FRED. Hey I didnae see you suckin his dick.

STEW. That's fuckin inappropriate Fred. I was trying to put him in the picture.

FRED. Me too.

STEW. Aye so you were.

FRED. In ma own way. (FRED*'s mobile rings.*) All right man? What you up to?

STEW. Who is it?

FRED. Cheesy.

STEW. Fuckin wido.

FRED. He's right here. His battery's flat.

STEW. What's he after?

FRED. He wants to talk to you. (*Hands mobile to* STEW.)

STEW. What's up? What? Naw Gibby's back. Knocked on the door, I opened it, there he was. What about Malone? Naw I know what he thinks he saw.

Enter GIBB.

So anyway, you want me to come and meet you? Don't fuckin start with it Cheesy . . . Listen I'll meet you at the water fountain in fifteen minutes . . . naw man it's always up front. Well get it from Malone then. I'll tell him you said hello. (*Hangs up.*) Every fuckin time. (*Pause. To* GIBB.) If you want a shower have a shower.

GIBB. I'm fine, I just needed to wet ma face.

STEW. Right.

GIBB. I'll mibbe have a bath tonight.

STEW. Aye whatever you like.

GIBB. See how I feel. (*Pause.*) What's he sayin?

STEW. Who?

GIBB. Cheesy.

STEW. Nothin man, he's just after some gear.

FRED. Hey Stew, you better move your arse.

STEW. You're right yea . . . right I'm . . .

GIBB. He sounded like he was . . .

STEW. What?

GIBB. I dunno, it sounded like –

FRED. He's a fuckin wind-up merchant.

STEW. The guy never stops.

FRED. You mind what he was like.

GIBB. I think so.

STEW. I'll be off before I start climbing the walls. See you guys in a bit.

GIBB. See you mate.

FRED. Aye later Stew.

STEW. Jesus Christ guys, we need to celebrate Gibby's return, ay. I'll pick up a nice bottle of whisky from the offy an Fred'll knock us up some scran how's about it?

GIBB. Sounds good to me.

STEW. Good stuff. Fred, you don't mind do you?

FRED. Dinnae be daft. The least we can do is feed the cunt.

STEW. Nectar. We'll all get off our heads have a fuckin laugh, do some proper catching up.

GIBB. Nice one.

STEW. Yea, there's some things we need to get sorted out as well.

GIBB. Fair enough.

Pause.

STEW. It's good to see you Tone.

GIBB. It's good to be back.

STEW. See youse in a bit then.

GIBB. Aye laters mate.

STEW *exits.*

Pause.

FRED. I think it's been a bit of a . . . you know, a bit of a fuckin trauma for the boy.

GIBB. I dunno, seems like the same old Stew to me.

FRED. You know what he's like.

GIBB. Aye.

FRED. All or nothing.

GIBB. Aye.

FRED. Always was, always will be. Fair enough ay?

GIBB. Yea but at least you know where you are.

FRED. Aye I suppose there's nothing wrong with being predictable.

GIBB *opens the kitchen door.* FRED *gets a can of Red Stripe.*

You want a tin Gibb?

GIBB. What?

FRED. You want a beer?

GIBB. Me? No I'm all right man.

FRED. Well they're in the fridge if you do. (*Starts skinning up.*) What you doing?

GIBB. Nothing man, just checking out the garden.

FRED. Aye we kinda let it go once you fucked off.

GIBB. So I see.

26

FRED. Aye we never had the time did we?

GIBB. That's all right, it'll give me something to get stuck into. (*Exits. Offstage.*) Hey Fred.

FRED. What?

GIBB (*offstage*). The rhubarb.

FRED. What about it?

GIBB (*offstage*). I think it needs cutting back.

FRED. Naw we like it like that.

GIBB (*offstage*). Naw we need to cut it back, you can make some crumble or some jam or something.

FRED. Nah it's better like it is.

GIBB (*enters holding a large stalk of rhubarb*). Come on man it's a fuckin eyesore.

Pause.

FRED. You look as though you lost a bit of weight.

GIBB. You reckon?

FRED. I dunno you look a bit gaunt. You hungry?

GIBB. Naw I'm all right now actually.

FRED. Mibbe later?

GIBB. Aye mibbe. (*Exits out of kitchen door.*)

FRED. Hey Gibby.

GIBB (*offstage*). What?

FRED. D'you get any nice minge down there?

GIBB (*offstage*). What you saying Fred?

FRED. D'you get any nice minge down there.

GIBB (*offstage*). Ay?

FRED. Fuckin pussy.

GIBB (*enters*). Who you callin a fuckin pussy?

FRED. I'm sayin did you get any?

GIBB. Aw right . . . eh . . .

FRED. Well did you or did you no?

GIBB. I've no complaints.

FRED. It's meant to be hoachin down there ay? One of ma punters was saying the place is crawling with Oriental fanny, is that right?

GIBB. It depends where you go.

FRED. Did you get any?

GIBB. Did I get any?

FRED. Aye did you get your teeth into any Oriental bush?

GIBB. No I never as a matter of fact.

FRED. No?

GIBB. I know it's hard to believe but –

FRED. A good-lookin guy like you?

GIBB. I kinda got the feeling it was all spoken for.

FRED. Aye?

GIBB. It doesnae jump out at you. If you went there you'd know what I mean. It's no as easy as you think.

FRED. What for a guy with your looks, I'd a thought you'd be fightin them of with a shitty stick man. Mind you, it does help if you've got the patter ay? If you can talk the talk.

GIBB (*staring out of the kitchen window*). Ken something Fred?

FRED. Naw what's that?

GIBB. I havenae seen a cow for over a year man.

FRED. Aye well wait till you meet Stew's bird.

GIBB. They look happy don't they?

FRED. What the cows?

GIBB. Yea man, they seem contented . . . at peace.

FRED. What you can tell can you?

GIBB. Yea man, they seem at peace.

FRED. You know why that is don't you?

GIBB. No.

FRED. It's cos they're fuckin stupid. Am I wrong?

GIBB. Well I dunno if I'd put quite like that but . . .

FRED. Anyway fuck the cows, I mean not literally at least . . .

GIBB *yawns and stretches.*

You tired Gibby?

GIBB. I'm a wee bit stiff from the train journey.

FRED. Why don't you stretch out on the couch?

GIBB. I might do that actually.

FRED. Aye, make yourself comfy. (GIBB *reclines on the couch.*)
That's more like it ay?

GIBB. Aye man.

FRED. You need to relax. So anyway, how you feeling?

GIBB. About what?

FRED. I dunno, in general, now you're back, how d'you feel?

GIBB. How do I feel?

FRED. Yea. About being back in Fife.

GIBB. Gimme a chance Fred, I just got off the fuckin train.

FRED. Fuck it man I just want to know what's going through your
mind, you know. What's your plans?

GIBB. Plans. Jesus . . . Christ I dunno.

FRED. You're no gonna fuck off again are you?

GIBB. No course not.

FRED. I mean you'd tell us wouldn't you? You'd do us the
courtesy?

GIBB. Actually, I was thinking I might go to college.

FRED. Yea?

GIBB. Aye, you know, it's just a thought.

FRED. Just an idea?

GIBB. Aye it's just something I thought about.

FRED. Down in London?

GIBB. Yea you know when I couldnae see the wood for the trees
I'd try and focus on the future.

FRED. Right.

GIBB. Try and work out what I really wanted to do with my life.

FRED. And did you?

GIBB. No. But I think maybe college could be a start.

FRED. Right.

GIBB. Yea I think it's finally time I actually started to use my brain, you know, before it goes to sleep forever.

FRED. I get you. (*Pause.*) So what d'you think you're gonna do?

GIBB. At college? I dunno . . . something worthwhile.

FRED. I know what you're sayin. I get that too.

GIBB. It's not uncommon at our age.

FRED. You want some music on?

GIBB. Naw I'm all right just now . . . Stick some on if you want though.

FRED. Nah you're all right. Sure you don't want a wee munch? I mean I'm gonna cook up something special later but we got plenty stuff in the fridge if you want something to chomp on.

GIBB. I'm all right, but thanks for asking.

FRED. Dinnae be shy now.

GIBB. I won't.

FRED. I mean you can be quiet, but you don't need to be shy. This is your house, despite what I said earlier which was just ma wee joke for Jesus you know.

GIBB. I know.

FRED. Naw, I know you know, I'm just saying. (*Pause.*) So, since you're the kind of guest of honour, what you want me to make you for later? I tell you, I've really got the hang of the cooking lark mate, I just got into it when you went away. I think, I dunno, I think I needed some kind of diversion.

GIBB. Are those all your books?

FRED. Yea, I thought if I bought the books and record all the cooking programmes on the telly so I could try the recipes out in my own time.

GIBB. That's a fair few books you've got Fred.

FRED. Yea and they're no cheap either. I think I've got a natural talent for it you know . . . like green fingers, but in the kitchen as opposed to the garden.

GIBB. Aye that fuckin garden's a disgrace.

FRED. Seriously mate, I just need to open the cupboards or the fridge and I get this, this urge to create you know. I dunno what it is but show me some fresh veg and a decent piece of meat and I . . . I dunno it just surges right through me. (*Gets chicken fillets from the fridge.*) Check it out. Organic chicken fillets. Beautiful so they are. Don't you think?

GIBB. You want my honest opinion?

FRED. I don't want you to bullshit me.

GIBB. Oh aye they're handsome fillets that's for sure.

FRED. Look at that man. See?

GIBB. No what?

FRED. Look.

GIBB. What am I supposed to be looking at?

FRED. The price. Five-seventy-eight for four wee fillets. It's no cheap ye ken. Still you got to go with the organic when you can. You cannae be filling yourself full of that force-fed mass-produced shite. I'm gonna do you a chicken stir-fry. I tell you what you should see me with a wok. I'm the king of the wok these days. I saw it on the telly how to butterfly a fillet. See, you cut into the fillet here, open it right up, cut the boy into wee thin strips, so it cooks faster. Your veg is no gonna go soggy and for presentation purposes it's a winner all the way . . . Yea, I'll do you some chicken, you fancy it? A bit of chicken? I've got some red peppers, carrots, baby sweetcorn, mange-tout, a bit of broccoli, salt, pepper, good bit of garlic, bung it in on a high heat with some extra virgin, oyster sauce if you're that way inclined. Keepin it simple, Gibby. Simplicity, that's the key to the wok. So?

GIBB. Nah I'm okay just now.

FRED. Naw I mean for later you fuckin bozo.

GIBB. Oh.

FRED. Well you just say the word.

GIBB. Aye that sounds great Fred.

FRED. Yea well I'm gonna do it anyway. (*Pause.*) Christ I cannae believe you went to London without me. You know I always wanted to go to London.

GIBB. It's not like it was anything personal Fred.

FRED. Aye whatever . . . So what was it like?

GIBB. London? It was all right.

FRED. What did you get up to? What did you do?

GIBB. Worked mostly.

FRED. All right but did you go out, meet people?

GIBB. Yea but nothing special, nothing glamorous, I just kinda bummed about.

FRED. Bummed about? Right. What d'you mean bummed about?

GIBB. Nothin I just fucked around for a –

FRED. You fucked around? Sounds a bit seedy to me. (*Pause.*) You didnae get into any trouble or nothing?

GIBB. What kind of trouble?

FRED. I dunno you tell me.

GIBB. What are you getting at?

FRED*'s mobile rings.*

FRED. Hold on a sec.

GIBB. If you've got anything to say Fred . . .

FRED. I've got to take this.

GIBB. Just come right out and fuckin say it.

FRED. Cheesy. Naw he's got to go an get it first. Stay where you are . . . all right stick him on. Malone, yea . . . his battery's flat. Calm down Malone. I guarantee he'll be there in the next ten minutes okay? (*Hangs up.*) Cunts.

GIBB. Got any drugs Fred?

FRED. Ay?

GIBB. Got any drugs?

FRED. Does a gorilla have hairy balls?

GIBB. Got any in the house?

FRED. Got some bits and bobs likes. No want a smoke of the joint?

GIBB. Nah, you got any wizz?

FRED. What d'you want speed for?

GIBB. I dunno, clear the cobwebs.

FRED. Nah we stopped selling speed.

GIBB. Aye?

FRED. Aye speed's dead man, no money in it.

GIBB. Same in London.

FRED. Got some coke though.

GIBB. Aye?

FRED. Aye it's all coke nowadays man. You want some?

GIBB. Nah you're all right.

FRED. What's the matter with you?

GIBB. It doesnae really do it for me.

FRED. Get a line down you, it'll perk you up.

GIBB. You reckon?

FRED. Go for it.

GIBB. Aye goan then.

FRED. It's upstairs.

GIBB. Is it any good?

FRED. As good as it gets. Mind you I hardly touch the stuff. Plays havoc with ma bowels.

GIBB. Aye I might have myself a couple of wee lines.

FRED. Well it's upstairs if you want it.

GIBB. Whereabouts upstairs?

FRED. In my room, there's about a gram in a box by the table lamp.

GIBB. Nice one. So it's good stuff?

FRED. Oh aye it's quality gear man.

Pause.

GIBB. You want to go get it for us then?

FRED. You know where my room is.

GIBB. I know but . . .

FRED. Hey it's cool. I understand. It's like the return of the prodigal son ay? You got to expect at least a day's grace to find your feet an that.

GIBB. You know how it is.

FRED. Oh aye, I know how it is.

GIBB. Look I'll go up if it's any bother to you.

FRED. Sit the fuck down Gibby. I'm just . . .

GIBB. You sure?

FRED. Ocht aye, it's nae bother likes. (*Makes his way to the door.*) I have to admit it's strange seeing you again. Aye a bit fucked up like. You look different. I don't know what it is but there's something different about you. Something's changed. I think it's your face.

FRED *exits.*

Fade lights.

GIBB *gets up, sings to himself. Suddenly frustrated, he stops singing. Collapses back into his chair.*

GIBB. Get it to-fuckin-gether man.

Blackout.

Scene Two

GIBB *is snorting a fat line. He takes it back and washes it down with a vodka Red Bull.* FRED *has a big knife and is chopping the veg with aplomb.* GIBB *has a big snort, the coke catches his throat, he starts coughing.*

FRED. Good gear ay?

GIBB. Aye man fuckin quality.

FRED (*gives* GIBB *a glass of water*). Here, get that ben you.

GIBB. Ta man. So when d'you start puntin the charlie?

FRED. Aye when everybody decided they couldnae get enough of it . . .

GIBB. Aye?

FRED. We made sure we could.

GIBB. I hear you.

FRED. What can you do? Es are three quid a pop, the club scene's dyin on it's arse, speeds dead, it's forty quid an ounce for solids and grass takes up too much space. What you gonna do?

GIBB. Nah you gotta adapt like.

FRED. Aye or get a proper job. D'you like garlic?

GIBB. Aye I take a bit of garlic.

FRED. Good cos I'm bunging loads in.

GIBB. Fine by me.

FRED. Aye you can never have enough garlic.

GIBB. You having another line? (*Passes* FRED *the mirror.*)

FRED. Mibbe just a wee one. Gotta watch the appetite. By the way, I may as well tell you . . . a quarter of all the profits are yours. We thought that was a fair amount. (*Snorts line.*) No bad for doin fuck-all ay? I don't know exactly how much it comes to you'll need to ask Stew.

GIBB. Stew runs the business these days?

FRED. He likes to think he does.

GIBB. So you sayin you run the business?

FRED. No that's not what I'm sayin Gibby.

GIBB. What are you sayin Fred?

FRED. I'm sayin like all good businesses they run themselves an if Stew likes to think he's the big man then I just let him get on with it. But the real truth of the situation is . . . if we've got it folk'll buy it.

GIBB. So who's buyin?

FRED. Everybody.

GIBB. Aye?

FRED. Oh aye, it's all the same folk as before.

GIBB. Easy money.

FRED. Oh aye the money's easy, but . . .

GIBB. But what?

FRED. It's still a fuckin full-time job Gibby. We're still running up and down the length and breadth of the country five days a week. It's just a wee bit more pressure when you're a man short you know?

GIBB. I'm sorry about that.

FRED. So you should be. It's been a bit too hectic and what with everything else that's goin on.

GIBB. I never meant to –

FRED. Hey man, tell it to the fuckin judge. (*Pause.*) Listen Gibby, what's done is done, but, like we said before, the time in between . . . it doesnae stand still you know?

GIBB. I know.

FRED. I'm sure you do Gibb, you're a smart guy, I mean you always came across as being the deep one but . . . well you should know as well as anybody, things change mate. People change.

GIBB. It's only natural.

FRED. There's nothing sacred Gibby.

GIBB. I dunno if I'd go that far but –

FRED. I mean it, there's fuck-all set in stone Gibb. What if you'd have come back and the locks were changed ay? What if we'd have fucked off an gone our separate ways, you come back you wouldnae know what went down or fuck-all now would you?

GIBB. I had a feeling youse'd be here.

FRED. Oh did you?

GIBB. I did, yea.

FRED. How's that like?

GIBB. I dunno, I just didnae imagine you being anywhere else.

FRED. We're that fuckin predictable are we?

GIBB. Come on Fred, that's not what I'm getting at.

FRED. D'you think I've got no other ambition than to run round selling that shite for a living? I mean I cannae speak for Stew and to be honest with you I havenae got a fuckin clue what goes on in that boy's head these days but . . . there's other things I want from my life. I got some O' Grades too you know.

GIBB. I know you did.

FRED. And I've got hidden talents.

GIBB. I dare say you –

FRED. Maybe you cannae see them.

GIBB. Well I cannae see them if they're fuckin hidden Fred.

FRED. Ha fuckin ha Gibby, you been working on your repartee?

GIBB. Naw Fred I'm just –

FRED. I mean it. Most people are talentless fuckers, blagging their way through life till they're finally exposed. *(Pause.)* Example. Last week, I'm at this Italian restaurant in Edinburgh one of my clients recommended, so I thought fuck it, I'll give it a go. So I get there, nice place, I order the tagliatelle. I mean I'm talking tagliatelle here . . . meat, pasta and some fuckin sauce, a simple rustic dish. So it comes over, I stick my fork in and I'm like Christ what's goin on here? The pasta was overcooked, the sauce was too thick, stuck to the roof of your mouth, damn near made me gag right there.

GIBB. Aye?

FRED. Total fuckin train wreck, you know . . . there was no flavour, no seasoning . . . Fuckin let-down. So I grabbed the waiter an I says I want to speak to the chef an the waiter says the head chef was on holiday. So I says look mate, I want to speak to someone about the sauce, whoever's responsible for this fuckin shambolic display of . . .

GIBB. Did you say fuckin?

FRED. No but I did say shambolic.

GIBB. Good effort.

FRED. Yea I liked it too. But naw, I was totally polite. So this comis chef comes out an I tell him, I says mate, your pasta's fuckin rank an your sauce is like glue. He was just a young guy tryin to grow a goatee beard so naturally I assumed he's just a student. But no, turns out he did one of these intensive catering courses, in Mayfair in London and had, he assured me, a legitimate qualification. *(Pause.)* I'm like what, do they let any cunt in? An he says, well basically if you've got four fuckin grand they'll take you. I'm like . . . four fuckin grand, that's all it takes? I says mate, I've never been to no catering college but I'm telling you, if this was my kitchen, an that was your sauce, I'd kick you out that fuckin door so fast you wouldnae know if it was New York or New Year. *(Snorts line.)* Fuck me that's good gear.

GIBB. Aye so I see.

FRED. Was I on one?

GIBB. Just a wee bit.

FRED. I told you, I hardly touch the stuff.

GIBB. It plays havoc.

FRED. Aye like a train through a tunnel . . . Makes you think though. Four fuckin grand, and what with my natural talent and winning personality, I'm telling you, five years tops I'd have my own show.

GIBB. You reckon?

FRED. Easy as pie.

Pause.

GIBB. So how are things with you and Stew?

FRED. What can I say, there's acceptable levels of tension and friction in everyday life but . . .

GIBB. But what?

FRED. Well I'm no gonna spill my guts for you but, I dunno, it's like they say - two's company and three's a crowd. But sometimes you need a crowd. It gets fucked up when it's just the two. Still . . . He's got himself a woman now. (*Pause.*) I want to show you something. (*Gets a photo from the cupboard.*) Check it out, April 2003, this is the last photo of us together. There's a red photo album in the cupboard with all the best ones all carefully selected. I mean there's a load more, I've got some, he's got some, but the ones in there, these are supposedly the best. Two guesses whose idea it was.

GIBB. He chose them all?

FRED. Every last fuckin one.

GIBB. And you never helped?

FRED. You know me Gibb, I don't do nostalgia.

GIBB. Each to his own ay.

FRED. He thought he was never gonna see you again. Look. We all look different now, ay? Older, puffed out . . . well maybe no you but me and Stew definitely seem to be carrying a wee bit extra timber. Not you though. You always had a baby face. Don't ask me why but I was hoping you'd lose it.

Enter STEW. GIBB *snorts a fat line.*

STEW. I see you've started the party without me. Here.

38

Hands bottle of whisky to FRED, *then sits down next to* GIBB. FRED *inspects bottle.*

Is that all right for youse?

Chops out a line, GIBB *crosses over to* FRED.

FRED. That's more than all right. Here Gibb, check it out.

GIBB. Islay Malt. Nice one.

STEW. Do the job ay?

GIBB. Oh Fuck aye.

FRED. How d'you get on with Malone and Cheesy?

STEW. Cunts.

FRED. Yea . . . So?

STEW. Usual fuckin nonsense. Is that a joint in the ashtray? (*Picks up the joint, smells it.*) Nice one. (*Lights up.*)

FRED. So?

STEW. This is getting to be hard work.

GIBB. What is?

STEW. Eating shit on a daily basis.

GIBB. It's not good for you.

STEW. It's never good for you.

FRED. Hey fuck it man, they're just a couple of troublemakers. It's no big deal.

STEW. It is if they're making trouble for me.

GIBB. What they saying likes?

STEW. Usual shite. Malone wanted a quarter on tick. I told him he knew the score. He called me a tight-arse and what not so I tried to defuse the situation and made a couple of jokes. He laughed, but it wasnae a real laugh. It was something else.

FRED. So when d'you want to eat?

STEW. I dunno. Anyway, I told him. I said if I gave him tick I'd never see the cash again. He didnae like that.

FRED. Right . . . so d'you want to eat now or d'you –

STEW. No I don't want to eat just now, maybe later.

FRED. It's not a problem . . . I'll do it three quarters now, an heat it through later.

GIBB. Can you do that with chicken?

FRED. Tell him Stew.

STEW. Tell him what?

FRED. Tell him I'm the king of the wok.

STEW. Fuckin tell him yourself.

FRED. He doesnae believe me.

STEW. Is that right?

GIBB. I never said I didnae –

FRED. I think he's turned all cynical in his old age.

GIBB. I dunno where you get that from.

FRED. He thinks it's all talk.

GIBB. I never said a fuckin word.

STEW. Rest assured Gibby, there's no finer man with a wok in these parts.

FRED. Case dismissed.

GIBB. I never said fuck-all in the first place.

STEW. Well anyway, fuck all this maudlin shite I say we all get fuckin buckled. Fred can do his legendary and majestic stir-fry chicken and we'll cane this bottle. There's enough drugs here to fill a pharmacy so there's no fuckin excuses. (*He plonks a selection of drugs on the table.*) Let's get fuckin caned. Gibby, you can tell us about London. And, if there's anything you want to share with us or get off your chest . . .

GIBB. Like what?

STEW. Like whatever . . . What I'm saying is tonight's as good a night as any. And while we're at it me an Fred'll fill you in about our future plans for the business.

FRED. Aye what plans are these like?

STEW. The shit we talked about. What d'you reckon Gibby?

GIBB. Sounds good to me.

STEW. That's the spirit son . . . Come here a sec, let's have a wee look at you.

GIBB. See anything you like?

FRED. Excuse me.

STEW. There's fuck-all of you.

GIBB. Yea, I havenae been eating much for some reason.

STEW. Christ man, what you been doing down there?

GIBB. What d'you mean likes?

STEW. I mean have you been doing smack? You better no have been doing smack. Cos I promise you I'll kick seven shades of shite out of you if you've been doing smack.

Pause.

GIBB. Did you find your pills?

STEW. What?

GIBB. Your Valium?

STEW. What? Oh aye, aye I found them nae bother.

GIBB. And you feel a bit better now yea?

STEW. Ay?

GIBB. You've calmed down a bit.

STEW. I feel all right. In fact talking of pills how about we all neck a wee sweetie before dinner? Who's game?

FRED. Not for me.

STEW. Gibby, you having one? (*Necks a pill.*)

GIBB. Naw, I'll pass. Maybe later.

STEW. What the fuck's the matter with you guys? Fuck it.

FRED. Hey Stew.

STEW. What?

FRED. I was saying he was always the pretty boy. (*He gets the photo album.*) He was wasn't he, he was always the babyface?

GIBB. Well that's news to me.

FRED. When was the last time you saw this photo?

GIBB. A long time ago.

FRED. Look. (*Shows* STEW.)

STEW. Shit man what was that, that was my . . .

FRED. Eleventh birthday party.

STEW. Right. Fuck me check the bowl cuts on us.

GIBB. Is that Bobby Lumsden?

STEW. So it is. I forgot about him. Poor bastard.

He crosses himself. GIBB *follows suit.*

Hey Fred.

FRED. What?

GIBB. Show some respect.

FRED. Aw right. (*Crosses himself.*)

STEW. His maw used to cut ma hair.

FRED. I showed this photo to my girlfriend once, she thought you were like my wee sister. Course I put her right. I was like no that's one of my oldest and dearest friends you're looking at, were in the Boys Brigade together, played in the football team, did the milk round. An she was like, no he really does look like a girl. An I says, what d'you mean like? An she said . . . he's got feminine features. And you know what?

STEW. No what?

FRED. Upon further perusal . . .

GIBB. What?

FRED. I was forced to agree.

Blackout.

Scene Three

The table is strewn with drug-taking paraphernalia, the whisky is two-thirds gone, there are empty cans of Red Bull, Red Stripe and a half-full bottle of Smirnoff. A crackly tape-recording of a church organ playing the hymn 'Eternal Father Strong to Save'.

FRED, STEW *and* GIBB *are seated. Each has a glass of whisky. They sing:*

Eternal Father, strong to save,
Whose arm hath bound the restless wave,
Who biddest the mighty ocean deep
Its own appointed limits keep;
Oh, hear us when we cry to Thee,

For those in peril on the sea!
O Trinity of love and power!
Our family shield in danger's hour;
From rock and tempest, fire and foe,
Protect us wheresoever we go;
Thus evermore shall rise to Thee
Glad hymns of praise from land and sea.

The music ends, a thump from the speakers. They hold a solemn silence.

FRED. So that was that.

STEW. Aye that was that.

GIBB. Aye.

FRED. Our song.

STEW. One of our songs.

GIBB. Aye.

FRED. That was one of our songs.

STEW. No is . . . is one of our songs.

GIBB. Aye.

STEW. Gets you here ay. (*Points to chest.*)

GIBB. Fuck aye.

STEW. Bobby fuckin Lumsden.

FRED. Hell of an organ player.

STEW. God aye.

GIBB. Who'd have thought ay? Fuckin brain tumour at twenty-two.

STEW. Does yer heed in ay?

FRED. It usually does.

STEW. What?

FRED. Brain tumours.

Pause.

STEW. To us. (*He raises his glass.*) I said to us. (*The others raise theirs.*) To us, and all that's like us.

GIBB. There's no many.

ALL THREE. And they're all deed. (*They clink and drink.*)

STEW *fixes himself a line of coke,* GIBB *opens the kitchen door,* FRED *attends to the music.*

STEW. Check it out boys. We've got Es, coke, downers, the best grass going, some nectar whisky an it's all right here in front of us. We can go all night, coast on through the wee small hours and right into the morning if we want. There's no pressure, none. But, when we're all done with this . . . soiree, what I'm sayin is after we've slept, things are gonna change. (*He snorts his line.*) That's the way I'm seeing things right now. Things have to change.

FRED. Any requests?

GIBB. Wow look at that sky, you can actually see the stars. You'll never see a sky like that in London. Never see a sky as clear.

STEW. Aye I suppose you just take it for granted, don't you?

GIBB. An I miss all the wee beasties that get caught in the light.

FRED. Who's for some tunes?

GIBB. All the daddy-longlegs . . . And moths battering against the windows trying to get in.

FRED. Anybody . . .

STEW. Fred.

FRED. What?

STEW. Get a line ben you. Gibb, you too c'mon. (*Sorts out some fat lines.*) So, now we're back to full strength this is what I have to say. (*Clears the phlegm from his throat.*) Gimme me a sec. (*He grabs the bin, spits in it.*) Fuck me check that out. Christ that cannae be good for you.

GIBB. Better out than in though.

STEW. I dunno, looks like I got a wee bit of my lung crawlin about in there. Anyway . . . so, guys, what I'm saying is it's time for a change. A change of strategy, a change of business and a change of location.

FRED. What you on about?

STEW. Getting out of here before it's too late.

FRED. Aw for fuck sake man.

STEW. What?

FRED. Now's no the time for heavy shit, the cunt's just back.

STEW. No hear me out. I've thought about this a lot. Listen we're not dealers, we never were, never have been. Opportunists is the worst you could say about us. It came along, what? A chance. So we took it. We knew people, and we knew people who knew people and it's just snowballed. I mean we started so small we never even knew we'd started. But we've done fuck-all wrong and there's nothing to be ashamed of. Who's first?

FRED (*to* GIBB). After you.

GIBB *snorts a line.*

I'm not ashamed of anything.

STEW. And nor should you be.

FRED. I don't believe in shame. (*Snorts his line.*)

STEW. Listen. We don't come from the best families. Not the best, but then again not the worst. I cannae deny my parents' achievements are at best modest. But they brought us up, well enough to know right from wrong, to know the value of things and to give us a sense of integrity. Who's for another whisky? (*He pours three whiskys.*) I mean it was our decision to come here. Okay so we left some people behind but we all know what it was about. Self-preservation. We don't owe the folk here nothing, our only loyalty is to each other. Either way my mind's made up. You guys are like brothers to me. I only had a sister and she got out ages ago.

FRED. Aye but she was a lesbian.

STEW. Anyway, now it's time for me to fuck off.

FRED. Fuck off where likes?

STEW. Get the fuck out of Fife, with ma two wee brothers, the brothers I never had but I always wanted. Wee Gibby and wee Fred.

FRED. Less of the wee ay.

GIBB. So I take it I'm forgiven then?

STEW. It's not about forgiveness Tony.

FRED. What is it about?

STEW. I just told you.

FRED. No I mean in a nutshell.

STEW. We need to develop a kind of fortress mentality.

FRED. Meaning what like?

STEW. Meaning get ourselves a wee cottage in the middle of
nowhere, keep our heads down, make some fuckin money an
take it from there. Now come on, let's all have a wee snifter.
I propose a toast.

FRED. So eh, what we drinking to?

STEW. The future.

FRED. What the future in general or –

STEW. Our future.

FRED. But we don't know what it is.

GIBB. That kinda goes with the turf Fred.

FRED. What I mean is we haven't discussed our future.

STEW. That's what we're doing.

FRED. We're discussing now?

GIBB. I reckon now's as good a time as any Fred.

FRED. It sounded more like the fuckin sermon on the mount to me.

STEW. So why don't you tell us what you think Fred?

FRED. Well see I thought we were just drinking.

STEW. Yea, so we've drank to us, now we drink to our future.

GIBB. Hey Fred, c'mon man ay. (*Raising his glass.*) To the three of
us, to us and our future.

STEW. I'll drink to that.

FRED. Aye, an I'll drink too.

STEW. I'm fuckin glad.

FRED. But not to that since I don't know what it is.

STEW. Well I'll fuckin tell you.

FRED. You'll tell me the future?

STEW. After you drink.

GIBB. Guys am I missing something here?

FRED. I cannae believe it, I'm sharing a house with Mystic fuckin
Meg.

STEW. There's gonna be changes. Now drink. (*To* FRED.) I told
you about this.

FRED. You told me?

STEW. Aye.

FRED. When?

STEW. Lots of times. Now come on, get it ben you. We're drinking to the future.

FRED. I'm not.

GIBB. You won't?

FRED. No.

GIBB. Why not?

FRED. I've got my reasons.

GIBB. And?

FRED. And now is not the time.

GIBB. Guys. (*Pause.*) This is all a bit . . .

STEW. What?

GIBB. I dunno . . . it's a bit fuckin petty.

FRED. Aye well welcome home Tony.

GIBB. I dunno, maybe I thought we were above it.

Pause.

FRED. I tell you what I'll drink to. I'll drink to this malt whisky.

GIBB. You'll drink to the drink?

FRED. I'm gonna drink to the drink.

GIBB. Not the future?

FRED. Not yet, maybe later.

GIBB. Maybe later?

FRED. Maybe later when I know what it is.

GIBB. None of us know the exact fuckin future Fred.

FRED. Well this cunt seems to think he does.

GIBB. D'you no think you're being just a wee bit stubborn Fred?

FRED. Nope.

GIBB. So you're not gonna drink –

FRED. That's my final offer.

GIBB. There's surely got to be a way to sort this out . . . this is . . . this is nothing to do with me is it?

Pause.

STEW (*stands up*). Okay now this . . . this is a good whisky. Now I don't know much about whisky. I plan to, but at this point my knowledge of whisky is at best . . .

FRED. Rudimentary.

STEW. Check out Johnny Thesaurus in the corner.

FRED. It's just another word for basic.

STEW. So why didn't you just say basic?

GIBB. Naw fair's fair Stew, it's never a bad thing to have a good command of the language.

STEW. Oh right, help us out when we're lost for words.

FRED. That's what I'm here for.

STEW. Okay now look . . . I know a single malt from a blend. My Bells from my Grouse. My Whyte and MacKay from my Cream of the Barley. I know they make a fuck of a lot of whisky on Islay and who lives on Islay? About six people and they all own distilleries. But I know that if there's one thing we're famous for this is it, the contents of this glass. This, Sean Connery and the Loch Ness Monster and the Loch Ness Monster doesnae even exist, so I suppose that's really only two things. Every country in the world this is known as Scotch. The drink is named after the country. People ask for the country not the drink, they ask for a Scotch. Scotch on the rocks, Scotch and soda, Scotch and . . .

FRED. Irn-Bru.

STEW. No, I don't think they ask for Scotch and Irn-Bru Fred but I welcome your contribution.

FRED. I was taking the piss.

STEW. Y'see what I have to put up with? (*Pause.*) It's not called English and it's not called Chinese. But we call it whisky, so what does that mean? I dunno . . . but if we can't drink to the future we may as well be drinking G & Ts, Bacardi and Cokes, or a dry Martini with a fuckin cherry, an umbrella and a dildo up our arses. But we're not. No. This is a thirty-nine-pound bottle of whisky, paid for in good faith and I'm gonna raise my glass, in good faith to the future, and anyone else who has any objections can come and talk to me about it right now and I'll be happy to discuss it with them.

Pause.

FRED. You're not the boss. There's no bosses in this house. And guess what, this is not your show either. We can all take the floor. See look. I can take it. I can command the stage. You forget no one's looking, no one gives a shit. It's just us three and no one else. (*Raises his glass.*) I'll drink to the drink . . . I can see it's a single malt, I can read the label an I can read the bumf on the back of the bottle just the same as anybody else so I know you made an effort. Oh aye, I can see that this has got integrity so I'll drink to it, and anyone who cares to join me I'll drink with them. If not . . . I don't give a fuck. (*Pause.*) To the drink.

Silence.

GIBB. I think we got ourselves a stalemate here guys.

Pause.

STEW. I'm not proud. Okay I am proud but I'm not proud, not proud right now if you see what I mean . . . All I was sayin was there's things we need to discuss, there's things –

GIBB. Hey c'mon Stew.

STEW. What?

GIBB. Let's drink to the fuckin drink man.

FRED. Gentlemen. (*Raises his glass.*) To the drink.

GIBB (*raises glass*). To the drink.

STEW (*raises glass*). To the drink.

ALL. To the drink. (*They drink, hold the taste, the flavour, the moment.*)

FRED. So . . . who's for some grub then? Speciality of the house? Stir-fry chicken, what d'you say Gibby? (*Goes to the cooker, turns gas on, rubs a half clove of garlic round side of wok, pours in oil.*)

GIBB. Aye I'll take a wee bit.

FRED. Good man. Stew. You'll be takin some won't you?

STEW. Eh . . . I dunno.

FRED. You don't know? Come on man, I already seared the chicken, all I need to do is blast it with the fuckin veg.

STEW. I dunno, you guys have some.

FRED. Come on man, I made it for all of us.

STEW. You having some Gibby?

GIBB. I think it'd be rude not to.

FRED. That's what we like to hear. And Gibby, I give you my own personal guarantee that you will not be disappointed.

GIBB. I'm looking forward to it.

FRED. See what I did with the garlic there Gibby? That's a wee trade secret . . . gives it a wee edge. Keep it to yourself.

GIBB. Right-oh Fred. (*To* STEW.) I hear you've got a girlfriend.

FRED. I told him.

GIBB. What's she like?

STEW. Aye she's all right like.

FRED. So now we've got the wok on some serious heat because of course the hotter the pan, the crunchier the veg. And then we bung in the veg and season. Never be afraid to season, now who said that?

GIBB. What's her name?

FRED. Delia.

STEW. Celia.

FRED. It was Delia. Fuckin hell man.

STEW. Her name's Celia.

FRED. Delia Smith said you should never be afraid to season. What's with this Celia nonsense?

STEW. My girlfriend.

FRED. Oh. Aye his bird's called Celia.

GIBB. Celia.

STEW. Aye Celia.

GIBB. That's a nice name. So . . . fill me in, what does she do with herself and where's she from?

STEW. Near Inverness.

GIBB. Oh you got yourself a highland girl?

FRED. Nah both her parents are English.

GIBB. Oh right.

STEW. Aye they sold up and got out of London when she was young.

GIBB. Obviously got a bit of cash then ay?

STEW. Aye they own a hotel and a coffee-shop in Nairn.

GIBB. So how d'you meet her?

STEW. A party at Philly Millar's.

GIBB. Fuck me, Philly Millar what's he up to?

STEW. Same as ever, sound guy but he still thinks he's the don.

GIBB. He was a good guy, be nice to see him.

STEW. You will, we see him every other week. Anyway Celia and Philly's bird went to the same college, that's how they –

FRED. Okay, here we go. A wee bit oyster, a wee bit soya, and then we toss the fucker. (*Tosses stir-fry.*) You gotta know how to toss a stir-fry. You can stir it but it doesn't have the same effect. It's all in the wrist. See, you need flexibility.

STEW. So you fancy a trip up the highlands?

GIBB. You don't know how much mate.

FRED. It's all about having the finesse to commit to it. Look. Look at that. Did you see that? See how it turns itself round. Like fuckin magic.

STEW. I'm heading up the A9 on Monday.

FRED. You gotta give everything equal time in the heat. The last thing you want is soggy veg. It's an art so it is.

STEW. We'll take a trip up North, see some old friends.

GIBB. Sounds good to me.

FRED. Look at that. That's fuckin beautiful. You see them doing it on telly and you think it's a pose, you think they're fuckin cocktail chefs and yea, some of them are but generally speaking it's all for a reason. Oh my god this boy's got the touch. Check him out.

STEW. Hey Fred, you want another whisky?

FRED. Jesus Christ can you no see, I'm busy? And now we're ready to plate it up. Fuckin poetry so it is. (*Takes plates to the dinner table.*) All right boys let's have your skinny arses at the table.

GIBB. So, you an Celia, is it love?

FRED. It's getting fuckin cold come on.

GIBB. We're coming.

GIBB *and* STEW *cross to dinner table.*

STEW. I like her but, I dunno.

GIBB. Where is she now?

STEW. In bed.

FRED. Hey guys, this ain't the time for girl talk. There we go, get it down you. Look at those colours. Isn't that beautiful?

GIBB. I'm not really that hungry anymore Fred. I thought I was.

FRED. Oh. Did you eat on the train?

GIBB. I never eat on trains.

FRED. Must be the coke then.

GIBB. Must be.

FRED. Well just you eat what you can.

GIBB. I'll do my best.

FRED. What else can you do? (*Tucks in.*) Oh my God. That is absolute fuckin perfection. I couldn't have done it better. What d'you think?

GIBB. Yea it's nice.

FRED. What d'you think of the veg? Mange-tout and the sweetcorn work well together don't they? That's what you're looking for. Nutrition, refreshment and your vitamins all present and correct. Red veg with the B12 to attack the free radicals, and garlic for the blood, it's all there in what, off an on, ten minutes, nae fuckin bother.

STEW *leaves the dinner table, sits on sofa and skins up.*

And of course you've got the chicken, the chicken's got the protein and it's the protein that gets rid of the hunger. People think it's the carbs but the carbs just fill you up. Oh aye, that's nice and tender. Of course chicken's a meat you can never take for granted. Undercook it and you'll run the risk of salmonella, overcook it and all you've got are lumps of dry tasteless meat. But if you know what you're doing . . . and course I don't want to blow my own trumpet but I'm sure that's fairly obvious by now . . . (*To* STEW) What's up with you?

STEW. Nothing.

FRED. Gibby.

GIBB. What?

FRED. What the fuck is Stew doing?

GIBB. Don't you know?

FRED. Indulge me.

GIBB. Skinning up by the looks of it.

FRED. And why is he doing such a thing when I set before him a culinary masterpiece?

GIBB. I don't know.

STEW. I'm not hungry.

FRED. Did you hear him say for me to cook?

GIBB. Yea but . . .

FRED. And we would all drink whisky and talk and eat chicken?

GIBB. Yea but –

FRED. And, am I wrong but was this not in some way supposed to be a special meal, symbolic in some way of our friendship?

GIBB. Yea but we never twisted your arm or nothin.

FRED. No that's true, it's no secret I like to create.

GIBB. You're the one who said you were the king of the wok.

FRED. You're right I did say that.

GIBB. So is that not enough, to get the opportunity to show us your skills and sample your wares?

FRED. I think there's a wee bit more to it than that Gibb.

GIBB. Whether we eat the food or not is kind of irrelevant if we both fully understand and appreciate the gesture.

FRED. Oh . . . you're getting awfy philosophical now Gibby.

GIBB. An I mean, well what can I say but I for one am moved.

FRED. You're also talking out your arse.

GIBB. An I know I've only had a wee taste, but it is without a doubt a fuckin sublime stir-fry.

STEW. I don't need to taste it to know how good it is.

FRED. That's not the fuckin point and you know it.

GIBB. Stew's well aware you put your heart and soul into that chicken.

FRED. Gibby Gibby Gibby, what can I say? You've been away, you cannae be expected to know everything. But there's certain things that are just set in stone these days and if I go to the effort of creating a work of art, even if it is a ten-minute work of art for your undereducated palates I expect –

STEW. For fuck sakes Fred my fuckin appetite's gone.

FRED. That's not my problem.

STEW. An it's nae bother to me either.

FRED. You know your trouble? Filling yourself full of that shite.

STEW. No, I'm just not hungry at this moment in time Fred.

FRED. Coursing round your system. Eating away at you from the inside.

STEW. FRED.

FRED. What?

STEW. Quit being a cunt right. I'm not hungry. It's my choice.

FRED. EAT THE FUCKIN CHICKEN.

STEW. No.

FRED. Eat The Fuckin Stir-Fry.

STEW. I'm rolling a joint.

Pause.

FRED. What would you say if I said I was offended?

STEW. I'd say that was your choice.

FRED. In other countries people eat to celebrate. Italians. If we were Italian we'd all be round that table eating the family's own special risotto drinking red wine from the local vineyard and biting into big hunks of bread doused in olive oil from the . . . from the finest Tuscan olive groves.

GIBB. How do you know the finest olive groves are in Tuscany?

FRED. Any fool knows the best olives come from Tuscany. I'm talking about the return of a long-lost friend. This . . .

STEW. Gibby are you offended?

FRED. This fuckin cunt here is our long-lost friend.

STEW. Gibby, are you offended.

GIBB. Well to be honest . . .

FRED. He's too good-natured to be offended.

STEW. No but are you?

GIBB. I've seen worse.

FRED (*to* STEW). Who cooked the fuckin food?

STEW. Questions like that Fred, I'm not even going to dignify with an answer.

FRED. Eat.

STEW. No.

GIBB. Guys.

FRED. At least make an effort, at least even pretend to make an effort.

STEW. No.

FRED. One piece, please before it goes dry.

STEW. Stop being a fuckin cunt Fred.

FRED. Get it fuckin ben you. I don't care how. Force it down. Even if you fuckin choke on it just get it fuckin ben you or I mean it, I'll fuckin pan you with my wok. (*Gets the wok.*)

GIBB (*laughing*). Is this for real?

FRED. You're asking me if I'm for real? You don't know the half of it Gibb. You don't know how lucky you were to get out when you did. Even though a slight indication of your impending absence would have been if not acceptable at least courteous. However, this guy on the other hand, he's shat the fuckin bed.

STEW. Give it a fuckin break Fred.

FRED. It happened after you left. He's shot to fuckin bollocks. Take a look at him. What can I say that can't be seen with even the least educated of eyes? He's become completely unbalanced. And why? Well, there's only so many explanations but one thing's for sure, things was a lot better before . . .

STEW. Before what?

FRED. You know what I'm talking about.

STEW. I haven't a fuckin clue what you're talking about. (*Pours himself a whisky.*)

FRED. Eat a bit of chicken. (*Knocks whisky out of* STEW's *hands.*) See what I mean, you can drink but you cannae eat. No wonder this country's gone to the fuckin dogs.

FRED *takes a swipe with the wok,* STEW *dodges it.*

Eat the stir-fry you fuckin low-life piece of shite or I swear to God, I will, I'll pan you. I mean it, I'll pan your fuckin lamps in.

Has another swipe, STEW *dodges it.*

GIBB. Guys. Fred, what the fuck's this all about man? Guys . . . come on . . . we're better than this Fred.

GIBB *tries to move* FRED *away from* STEW. FRED *shrugs him off, knocks him to the floor,* STEW *is looking up at* FRED *who stands motionless, wok poised in his hand. Slowly fade lights.*

I thought we were celebrating.

FRED *swings at* STEW, *connects with his head and knocks him out cold.*

FRED. Back of the net.

GIBB. What the fuck is going on?

Blackout.

Scene Four

STEW *lies prostrate on the sofa, practically motionless, eyes open.* GIBB *examines him, then goes to the kitchen area and starts rummaging through the drawers and cupboards.* FRED *sits on the armchair with the wok on his head.*

FRED. If the Martians came down to earth there's every chance they'd look like this. Just like normal people with woks on their heads. I'm not actually saying they'd look like humans or anyone would mistake them or that they would even have woks on their heads . . . I'm just saying the object it would most resemble would be a wok. What?

GIBB. Nothing.

FRED. Yea and the handle of the wok would be like the antennae. What the fuck's the matter with you?

GIBB. I dunno, what the fuck is the matter?

FRED. You're giving me this funny look.

GIBB. Am I?

FRED. Yea. I don't like it.

GIBB. Sorry. Is this better?

FRED. Aye.

GIBB. Thank fuck for that.

FRED. Anyway . . . they would use their antennae to receive and transmit signals to an from the mother ship.

GIBB. It wouldnae just be the mother ship.

FRED. What?

GIBB. There would be other ships.

FRED. What other ships?

GIBB. Other ships other than the mother ship.

FRED. Don't be fuckin soft Gibby.

GIBB. There has to be . . . there has to be smaller ships, that can dock inside the mother ship otherwise why d'you call it a mother ship?

FRED. What you gibbering about?

GIBB. Okay why d'you think it's called the mother ship?

FRED. I dunno . . .

GIBB. What d'you think?

FRED. It's obviously cos it's the biggest ship.

GIBB. Which would suggest that there are other smaller ships inside the mother ship. And if you were gonna land on earth it'd be a lot safer to use one of the smaller ships don't you think?

FRED. Hold on a minute . . . now what I'm saying is –

GIBB. Fuck it, I don't even care. Do we have any bandages in the house?

FRED. What's all this you come back from London and you're an expert on science fiction all of a sudden?

GIBB. It's just common sense. Did we not used to have a red box with bandages and stuff in it?

FRED. There's a first-aid box in the cupboard under the stairs. Anyway as I was saying, once they'd got down there . . .

GIBB. How did they get down there?

FRED. In the fuckin mother ship.

GIBB. Nobody would notice if this huge mother ship landed –

FRED. They'd be beamed down all right.

GIBB. Aw right, like in Star Trek?

FRED. Exactly.

GIBB. They'd have some Martian guy like Scottie who could just twiddle a few knobs, press a few buttons and that'd be it?

FRED. Piece of piss.

GIBB. Some kind of anti-gravity, anti-matter device that could transport matter from one place to the next place in the blinking of an eye?

FRED. Aye.

GIBB. That's what you think?

FRED. I'm trying to tell you, if you'd just let me.

GIBB. Personally, I'd be a lot happier if you helped me get this cunt sorted out. (*Exits.*)

FRED. Not until I get to expound my theory. Anyway the first thing they'd do once they got down here however the fuck they got down here would be to look for somebody who knew how to cook a decent meal. That's the first thing a Martian would want . . . quality nosh. I mean I think that's blindingly obvious seeing as they've come such a long way. (FRED *snorts a line.*) You want a line Gibb?

GIBB (*offstage*). No thanks.

FRED. After that it's all open to interpretation, but I reckon after they'd loaded up on the grub they'd probably want to sample the local talent. Course, I could be way off the mark.

GIBB *enters with red first-aid kit.*

The Martians or whatever extra terrestrial beings who made it down here first, for all we know, as a race they might be serial monogamists, might be the most faithful, loyal, loving creatures in the universe but . . .

GIBB. I need a pair of scissors. (*Looks in cupboards.*)

FRED. But, it's my considered opinion that their thoughts would turn to the possibilities of procreation. They'd be looking to score a decent bit of earthling pussy. I'm assuming of course that most of them would be of the male gender. I mean their exploration party may well be split fifty-fifty. Like I say it's just my opinion, you can take it or leave it, personally I don't give a flying fuck. I don't care a fuckin jot.

GIBB. Are you done?

FRED. Yea, I'm done. (*Pause.*) Oh Christ I think that chicken's gone right through me.

GIBB. All right we need to put this bandage round his head.

FRED. You're no gonna use the whole bandage are you? I'm just saying first-aid kits dinnae come cheap.

GIBB. That's why I was looking for the scissors.

FRED. They're in the fuckin box. Have you got them?

GIBB. Yea. Okay you hold it here an make sure it doesnae slip.

FRED. Ken something, I dunno what's wrong with this cunt.

GIBB. You just fuckin panelled him with a wok.

FRED. No I admit that that's maybe a major factor in the fact that the guy's lying there fuckin cabbaged.

GIBB. Oh . . . good to see you're taking some responsibility.

FRED. Aye but aside from that, you got to admit he had it coming. Anyway I don't know what his problem is cos there's fuck-all in these pills, no MDMA that's for sure. Not like it used to be. Two or three sweeties and check the cut of him. (*To* STEW.) What are you good for? Ay. Nothing. No good for loving that's for sure.

GIBB (*cuts and ties the bandage*). Far be it from me to state the obvious Fred but I dinnae think battering him on the head with the wok's done him any favours.

FRED. Yea well I still say he had it fuckin coming. (*Pause.*) Fuckin pills. They don't even call them Es any more. I remember, when it used to be fifteen quid for an E, now it's like three fuckin quid, what's that all about? Yea you get out your face, I mean check this cunt out but it's not the buzz you're looking for is it?

GIBB *tries to prop up* STEW, *who keeps keeling over.*

Cos see if we had real MDMA, and we'd necked a couple of the buggers we'd all strip off and fuck each other right now. You know, really get to know each other, really fuckin catch up on things. We'd have no choice man, the drug would make us warm and tactile, make us want to touch each other. Make us explore our gay side. We've all got one, so I've read. I mean, I'm not gay, that goes without saying but it doesn't mean I haven't got a gay side. I'm as straight as it comes. Christ the Romans couldn't build roads as straight as the road my sexuality walks down . . . what I mean is, I've never looked at another guy and thought, what if, or maybe, or even considered it . . . but how can I be sure? I cannae actually say for sure, if it's in us all.

A knock on the door.

What the fuck was that?

GIBB. I'm guessing here but I'd say it was the door.

FRED *grabs the wok, goes out to the hall and stands poised by the front door, wok in hand. Another knock.*

What the fuck you doing with that?

FRED. Ay?

GIBB. The wok . . .

FRED. What?

GIBB. You don't even know do you?

FRED. It could be the DS.

GIBB. Yea, so what they gonna do break the door down?

FRED. Sshh.

GIBB. What?

FRED. You hear that?

GIBB. What?

FRED. I dunno. I'm telling you some cunt's tipped off the DS.

GIBB. What like who?

FRED. I don't think you fuckin get it Tone.

GIBB. Get what?

FRED. We're not fuckin popular here.

A firm knock. GIBB *starts clearing the drugs from the table.*

That's a fuckin polis knock I'm telling you . . . What you doing?

GIBB. I dunno I just got this sudden urge to tidy up.

FRED. Nah fuck that, if it's the DS they'll no be looking for personal, they'll be looking for our fuckin stash.

GIBB. Right . . .

FRED. Yea man . . .

GIBB. And where's the stash?

FRED. What don't you know?

GIBB. Excuse me but I'm a wee bit out of touch.

FRED. You're right I forgot . . . sorry.

Pause.

GIBB. So where's the stash?

FRED. Not here.

GIBB. So we're all right then.

FRED. I fuckin hope so.

GIBB. Good . . . We do have a stash though don't we?

FRED. Yea, well of course we got a fuckin stash.

GIBB. Right, so as a partner in the business, this is information that I would expect to be . . .

FRED. What?

GIBB. The whereabouts of our . . . Jesus man, where do we keep the fuckin shit, could you please kindly elucidate?

FRED. Elucidate . . . I like it.

GIBB. So . . . ?

FRED. All the shit gets kept at Celia's.

GIBB. Does she mind?

FRED. I dunno, ask her.

GIBB. I'm asking you.

FRED. She's got a flat on the other side of town which we pay for. Oh aye, she's well looked after.

Another knock.

Christ man when they gonna fuck off? It's startin to do ma head in.

GIBB. It doesnae help having the lights on.

FRED. Maybe we're out.

GIBB. Yea but we're not out are we?

FRED. Maybe we went out and left them on as a precaution. I mean that's standard procedure these days, what with all the –

Another knock.

GIBB. You know something?

FRED. What?

GIBB. I don't think it's the pigs.

FRED. How come?

GIBB. Cos I reckon they'd have said something imaginative like 'open up it's the police.'

FRED. Maybe they're trying to deceive us. Trying to lull us in. (*Pause.*) Shit man, what if that is the DS and they do actually have a warrant? They break the fuckin door down, go through every room in the house . . . Dig up the garden, make the whole place look like fuckin Beirut just cos they feel like it and all we can do is stand here and wait.

GIBB *creeps towards the hallway.*

Where you going?

GIBB. I'm gonna go upstairs an check it out.

FRED. I'm coming with you.

GIBB. Don't tell me you're scared Fred.

FRED. Sshh.

GIBB. What?

FRED. Keep your fuckin voice down.

They exit. Their whispered conversation continues offstage.

MALONE *enters through the kitchen door. Goes over to* STEW, *waves his hands in front of* STEW's *open yet glazed eyes, he gets no response. Pours himself a glass of whisky, smooths out a line of coke, takes it over to the dinner table. Tucks into* STEW's *uneaten food.*

GIBB *and* FRED *enter.*

GIBB. Well whoever it is or whatever it was there's nobody there now so . . .

FRED. What?

GIBB. Do you know this guy?

MALONE. All right boys. (*Pause.*) By the way, this is some tasty shit you've got here. (*Pause.*) As you can see I let myself in. (*Pause.*) Oh yea, you guys should really think about keeping that back door of yours locked. (*Snorts line.*) I'm telling you, any cunt could get in. Slange. (*Necks whisky.*)

FRED. I don't fuckin believe it.

MALONE. Fuckin hell that's good whisky. I telt Stew I'd mibbe pay youse a visit. Did he no say?

GIBB. No he didn't.

MALONE. So, youse've been celebrating then.

FRED. You cannae just go barging into people's houses Malone.

MALONE. You must be Gibby.

FRED. He's fuckin ignoring me.

MALONE. Sean Malone, pleased to meet you.

GIBB. You too.

MALONE. So what's it like being back?

GIBB. What's it like? Fuck, I dunno . . .

MALONE. Hey man look, I'm just making conversation.

GIBB. It's . . . it's great to be back.

FRED. I'm stunned, I mean it, I'm fuckin bewildered.

STEW *groans and convulses slightly.* GIBB *tends to him.*

MALONE. So what's up with your mate?

GIBB. Stew?

MALONE. Aye, what's his problem?

GIBB. I'm not exactly sure to be honest.

FRED. I dunno . . . people think they can just waltz into folks' houses, encroaching on a man's personal space and that's meant to be all right.

MALONE. Fred . . . You're a fuckin drug dealer.

FRED. And what exactly does that mean?

MALONE. It means all bets are off mate.

FRED. So I'm not entitled to the same basic liberties as the rest of the world is that what you're saying?

MALONE. Something along them lines.

Pause. GIBB *gets a wet cloth and wipes* STEW's *brow.*

FRED. Yea well at least I'm not a convicted rapist.

MALONE. It was attempted rape.

FRED. I stand corrected.

MALONE. Forget it it's not important.

FRED. No but I'll tell you what is important, is the two years they shaved off your sentence when you got parole. Two years they'd be happy to stitch back on if they found out that a convicted rapist –

MALONE. I'm no gonna tell you again Fred.

FRED. Okay, attempted rapist. Either way, it's still gonna fuck up your parole if it got out that you're hanging around with . . . what term did he use Gibby?

GIBB. He said we were drug dealers.

MALONE. Which is what youse are is it no?

FRED. Yea, but not convicted drug dealers. Which puts us a wee bit further up the food chain if you don't mind.

MALONE (*munching away*). Fuck me this is quality grub.

FRED. You think so? (*Joins* MALONE *at the dinner table.*)

MALONE. Yea man . . . damn fuckin tasty.

FRED. Good, well I'm glad somebody likes it.

MALONE. Did you make it yourself?

FRED. I certainly did.

MALONE. Fair fuckin dues Fred. It's a . . . it's a taste sensation, that's what it is.

FRED. That's organic chicken you're eating by the way.

MALONE. You're kidding?

FRED. Taste the difference can't you.

MALONE. Now you come to mention it I think I can. You know I had a serious case of the munchies when I left the pub and I wasnae exactly enamored by the choice available to me, you know, grease from the chippie or shit in a tray from the Chinese.

FRED. No choice at all is it?

MALONE. No, I'm fuckin glad I held out. So how come none of you guys are eating?

GIBB (*wiping drool from* STEW'*s face*). We got a bit distracted.

FRED. Yea we don't normally get visitors this late.

MALONE. So you panicked a wee bit didn't you?

FRED. I wouldnae go that far.

MALONE. You're probably thinking who the fuck knocks on the door at . . . what time is it by the way? Gotta make sure I catch last orders. Nice watch you've got there Fred.

FRED. Yea I like it too, that's why I bought it.

MALONE. How much you selling it for?

FRED. Fuck-all.

MALONE. You'll let me have it for nothing.

FRED. It's not for sale.

MALONE. You gotta try . . . So what time is it?

FRED. The time is now . . . ten to eleven.

MALONE. Nice one. Anyway I figured since nobody was gonna come to the front door what the fuck, I'll go round and see if I cannae get some joy with the back door. You sure he's all right?

FRED. He's fine.

MALONE. Something happen?

FRED. He banged his head.

MALONE. Must have been some bang.

GIBB. It was wasn't it Fred?

MALONE. Just as well he's got somebody to nurse him ay Gibby.

FRED. Excuse my rudeness but what's so important that you have to drag yourself from the pub to pay us a visit? I'm assuming this isnae a social call.

MALONE. Actually I come here out of the goodness of my heart.

FRED. Well that's a fuckin comfort.

MALONE. I've come to make you an offer.

FRED. Make me an offer?

MALONE. All three of you.

FRED. You're gonna make us all an offer?

MALONE. That's what I said.

FRED. Is it a special offer?

MALONE. Don't take the piss Fred. Look, I know you guys aren't stupid an I'm no here to take the piss out of you so –

FRED. Now hold on a sec . . . If letting yourself into someone else's house . . . helping yourself to their food, their drink and their drugs isnae taking the piss then by all means tell me what is, cos I thought I had a pretty fair idea you know.

GIBB. Guys. (*Pause.*) I said guys.

FRED *and* MALONE. What?

GIBB. We're a man down here. Look I know I'm not a doctor but –

FRED. There's fuck-all wrong with him.

GIBB. I'm starting to get a bit concerned.

FRED. He's fine.

GIBB. He's looked better though wouldn't you say?

MALONE. Any fuckin idiot can see he's looked better.

GIBB. We're gonna have to do something.

FRED. You've kinda come at a bad time Malone. I dunno maybe if you'd made an appointment we could have slotted you in but . . .

GIBB. Yea, you know mibbe give us a call tomorrow, come round when we're on a bit more of an even keel that might be –

MALONE. I don't think you guys realise . . . it's Friday night, an I've just left a pub heaving with boys who are all tanked up an high as fuckin kites and not one of them thinks youse cunts are any better than the shite they'd scrape of their shoes. You get what I'm saying we're talking unpredictable elements here. I'm talking about a load of loose cannons waiting to go off. (*Pause.*) So it's lucky for you guys that I've come here on their behalf.

FRED. Like a spokesperson?

MALONE. Exactly.

FRED. A delegate even.

MALONE. Aye . . . I've been delegated to come here an talk to you guys an make youse an offer. And I know it might seem hard to believe but I am actually doing this for your benefit.

GIBB. Okay, point taken, but before I can relax and listen to anything you have to say I have to make sure my friend's all right, if you want me to be receptive . . . cos obviously there's a good reason for you being here and I don't want to break the spirit of good will but –

MALONE. You don't fuckin get it do you?

GIBB. Hey mate we're doing our best.

FRED. Yea quit with the speeches Malone, tell it like it –

MALONE. See if I wanted I could have this house burned down by tomorrow. I can walk out that door, and guarantee you that by morning this cosy wee cottage wouldnae be much more than a smouldering heap of dust.

FRED. Are you threatening us?

MALONE. What d'you think? (*Pause.*) Now I can do that, and I will do that, but, to be honest with you, I don't want to do that kind of stuff anymore. It tires you out and you know something else, it gets a bit boring. So, I want to keep it as a last resort. So let's act like grown-ups ay?

Pause.

FRED. See the minute someone starts giving me ultimatums I have a tendency to switch off, I cannae help it, it just washes over me. I'm no daft Malone, I know you're a mad cunt. So if you're gonna do something do it, an if not . . . don't. Just spare me the idle threats.

MALONE. Okay, it's dead simple. There's roundabout thirty guys in the pub baying for your blood, crying out for some crude form of local justice. They want youse out the town and they don't give a fuck what they have to do an that's the end of it. Basically you've overstayed your welcome.

FRED. What fuckin welcome is this?

MALONE. Well look, I don't claim to know the full story cos I was . . . away for while but the gist of it seems to be . . . You come to the town, make no effort to get along. You set up shop and you sell your fuckin drugs, which okay, it's not a crime . . . well it is a crime but it's not, you know . . .

GIBB. We know what you mean.

MALONE. You know, it's the law of the jungle, you do what you have to do. But there comes a time when things boil over, when people say enough's enough . . . and tonight happens to be that night . . . Lucky for you guys they all look up to me.

FRED. No exactly a glowing endorsement though is it?

MALONE. Perhaps not but that's how it works. I'm the local radge. I'm the guy who's crashed cars, hit lassies and beat up Pakis. And no I'm not proud of that, but they all love me, fear me and respect me for it and d'you know why?

FRED. No why?

MALONE. Cos it means that none of them have to do it. They can tell stories in the pub about all the things I've done, their time passes just the same and they don't have to do fuck-all.

GIBB. Until now.

MALONE. But if I tell them all to shut the fuck up, they shut the fuck up. If I tell them to listen, they listen. Look, I'm no long out the jail and since I got out I've come to appreciate my freedom and see things in a different way. I've tried to turn over a new leaf. I dunno, to calm down, grow up.

FRED. Fuck me I'm choking back the tears.

GIBB. Can it Fred for fuck's sake.

MALONE. So I said I'd come and talk to you an see if I could maybe sort this thing out amicably. I said I'd give youse seven days to pack up an get the fuck out of here, and if you're okay with that then I would personally guarantee that fuck-all would happen to you.

FRED. You know what this is? This is small town fuckin bullshit.

MALONE. Aye but it's our small town Fred no yours.

FRED. Welcome to the fuckin Dark Ages.

MALONE. What d'you expect? You march into our town. You don't mix, you don't socialise and you don't pay your fuckin respects. No, you come across all aloof and superior. When Gibb disappeared what the fuck did you think was gonna happen? Of course you're gonna be the objects of ridicule. That's how it works. But you could've laughed along, rolled with the punches, used it as an opportunity to bond with some of the guys. When you're in the pub and everyone's making jokes about Gibby here maybe being a fuckin gay junkie rent-boy you coulda just went with it. (*Pause.*) It's not impossible for us all to get along you know. It's not like we come from the other side of the planet.

Pause.

GIBB. Junkie fuckin rent-boy . . . man that's harsh. I take it that's the rumors.

MALONE. Who says they're rumours?

FRED. So it is true?

MALONE. Ask your mate.

FRED. Gibby.

GIBB. What?

FRED. Is it true?

GIBB. Can we talk about it later please?

FRED. Just tell me that he's talking out his arse.

GIBB. I'm no really sure I can say that Fred.

FRED (*clutches his stomach*). Oh my God.

GIBB. You all right Fred?

FRED. I think I'll be talking out ma arse in a sec. Excuse me for a second guys but I need to get a load off my mind.

GIBB. I know how you feel.

FRED. No I mean I need to take a shit. (*Exits.*)

Pause.

MALONE. So you never told them?

GIBB. I was kinda waiting for the right moment.

MALONE. Aye, I suppose you cannae just walk in and say, 'Hi I've been in London suckin dicks for a living.'

GIBB. I never sucked any dicks.

MALONE. Either way I probably put my foot in it. It wouldnae be the first time.

GIBB. I wouldnae worry about it. We'd have got round to it sooner or later. Fuck knows how they found out though.

MALONE. I think Cheesy spread the rumors. He's like a fuckin radio . . . he receives, he transmits.

GIBB. How did he know?

MALONE. I told him.

GIBB. Who the fuck told you?

MALONE. I saw you. In London. I saw you at Kings Cross. About four or five months ago, no long after I got out.

GIBB. It's all a bit of a blur to be honest.

MALONE. You were smacked out your face. All over the fuckin shop.

GIBB. Aye that woulda been me.

MALONE. You asked me for money. I never knew who you were but I recognised the Fife accent. I gave you a fiver. You shook my hand, told me your name. Then a car pulled up, you got in. Some guy came up to me an asked me if I was looking for some company. I was gonna hammer him but I thought what the fuck's the point of that?

Pause.

GIBB. So if we agree to bugger off, then everything's cool?

MALONE. I'll give you my personal guarantee.

GIBB. An if we don't?

MALONE. Well I suppose I'd have to intervene.

GIBB. Why get involved?

MALONE. It's what's expected. I cannae let them down can I?

GIBB. What if you end up back inside?

MALONE. That depends on you guys . . . you know the rules. You dinnae want to be a grass now do you?

GIBB. What about your family?

MALONE. What can I say . . . In some ways I kinda like being the local radge. It's a small town, an at least I'm a somebody. If I hang up my spurs, what am I? I'm a fuckin nobody. A fuckin nobody in a small town who used to be a somebody. I cannae imagine anything worse than that.

GIBB. What happened to this new leaf you were turning?

MALONE. I said I tried . . . I'm still trying. It's no so easy with thirty guys cheering you on.

GIBB. So if we're here this time next week . . . what then?

MALONE. Well as long as you're awake when the fire-engines come you should be fine.

Enter FRED.

FRED. Tell me it's not true Gibby.

GIBB. I'd be lying if I said it wasnae.

FRED. You know we stuck our fuckin necks out for you Gibby.

GIBB. I know. I'm sorry . . . I'm really . . .

FRED. When I was up there having a shite all I could think of was you with some guy's cock in your mouth. Needless to say I threw up instantly an it wasnae pleasant if you get what I'm saying.

GIBB. I never sucked any cocks Fred, I just gave hand-jobs . . . if that's any consolation?

FRED. I cannae say it is to be honest.

STEW *exhales suddenly, burps, then spews a small amount of vomit. Then his body goes totally limp.*

GIBB. Guys we need to sort Stew out and I mean right now.

FRED. Don't look at me, I just do the food.

MALONE. Have you checked his pulse?

FRED. Did we check his pulse Gibby?

GIBB. Eh . . . no actually we never got round to it.

FRED. No we never checked his pulse.

MALONE. So what the fuck you waiting for?

FRED. I personally don't see what good it's gonna do.

GIBB. It's no gonna do him any harm is it?

FRED. All right fuck it, let's take the cunt's pulse.

MALONE. Do we have a volunteer? Come on. What's the matter with you guys?

GIBB. Right . . . Okay . . . I'm on the case. All right who's got a watch with a second hand? Fred.

FRED. What?

GIBB. Gimme a look at your watch.

FRED. Nah no chance this is an expensive watch.

GIBB. Has it got a second hand?

FRED. Aye but –

GIBB. Can I have it, please?

FRED. This is a two hundred-and-twenty-five quid watch mate, it never comes off ma wrist.

GIBB. D'you want to play doctor Fred?

FRED. I don't know how to, I told you I just –

GIBB. So then gimme the fuckin watch.

FRED. There's no need to fuckin swear at me . . . As long as I get it back.

GIBB. I'm no gonna nick it am I?

FRED. Look after it mind. (*Hands it over to* GIBB.)

GIBB. Nice watch. (*Takes* STEW's *pulse.*)

MALONE. What the fuck has actually been going on here Fred?

FRED. I dunno, what d'you mean?

MALONE. Your mate, with the bandage round his head who's just passed out.

FRED. I dunno. He was a wee bit caned, he stumbled, I never really saw it to be honest.

MALONE. Has he been taking drugs all night?

FRED. You know what the cunt's like.

MALONE. All right, what kind of drugs?

FRED. I dunno, I was busy –

MALONE. This stuff matters Fred. Okay . . . coke, you've all been doing coke yea? Now what else . . . pills?

FRED. He necked a couple of pills.

MALONE. Good, all right so we've got coke an pills. What else? Whisky, weed, beer, vodka, talk to me Fred.

FRED. I dunno, I was doing the food. Gibby.

GIBB. Shoosh I'm counting.

Pause.

FRED. When he went to get the coke he picked up some Valium.

MALONE. How many did you see him take?

FRED. I'm not his fuckin baby-sitter Malone.

MALONE. I just want to know roughly how many?

GIBB. Twenty-eight.

MALONE. Valiums?

GIBB. Beats. Here catch. (*Throws watch to* FRED.) He's fine.

MALONE. Twenty-eight?

FRED. That's a two-hundred quid watch you're flinging about.

GIBB. Just as well you caught it then ay.

MALONE. We need to get him to a hospital.

GIBB. He's all right trust me.

MALONE. Twenty-eight beats, the cunt's practically dead.

FRED. Gibby's the brains of the outfit an if he says he's fine, he's fine. Mind you twenty-eight is a bit –

MALONE. He could have had a brain haemorrhage.

GIBB. Look I counted to –

MALONE. Maybe he's already had one.

FRED. Hey hold on a minute.

MALONE. Look at him. Stuart. (*He tries to revive* STEW.)

FRED. Look we're having –

MALONE. Wake the fuck up.

FRED. There's gonna be no fatalities in this house.

MALONE. I'm calling an ambulance. (*Takes out his mobile.*)

FRED. Hold on a second, that's a bit extreme.

MALONE. Not if he dies an I'm here at the scene of the crime.

FRED. Nobody's fuckin dying, right.

MALONE. Hello . . . Yes, I'd like an ambulance please . . . What's the address?

FRED (*to* GIBB). Are you gonna do something?

MALONE. It's the cottage at the end of the estate . . . excuse me one second. Fred, what's the actual address of this place?

GIBB. Why don't you give me the phone and I'll talk to them.

MALONE. Just give me the fuckin address. (*To phone*.) I'm so sorry about this.

GIBB. He's fine.

MALONE (*to* GIBB). He's fuckin dying.

GIBB. Settle down Malone. I promise you, he's gonna be all right.

MALONE. How do you know?

GIBB. I only gave it half a minute, so if you multiply –

MALONE. What?

FRED. Nice one Tone.

GIBB. His heart rate's fifty-six beats a minute.

MALONE. Which means what?

GIBB. It means he looks like shit but he's safe as houses.

MALONE. So why the fuck didn't you say?

GIBB. I never got a chance.

FRED. Bit of fun there ay? Did you panic Malone?

GIBB. I promise you he's fine, he just needs to sleep it off. Trust me . . . I know a wee bit about first-aid. I've actually got a first-aid badge.

MALONE. Oh really.

GIBB. Seriously.

MALONE. Did you do a course or something?

GIBB. No I got one when I was in the BBs.

MALONE. And when exactly were you in the BBs?

GIBB. Well I left the BBs when I was fourteen but the first-aid badge I actually got when I was twelve. I'd forgotten all about it but when you said take his pulse it suddenly came back to me.

MALONE. This is a fucking joke isn't it?

GIBB. Not to me.

MALONE. You're trying to fuck with me aren't you?

GIBB. Not in the slightest, I'm proud of that badge.

FRED. So we're all done then. Christ I nearly had a heart attack myself there, and you know I've got a weak heart. I mean this cunt, (*Indicating* STEW.) he's generally got the constitution of an ox, but me –

MALONE. ENOUGH. (*Pause.*) The Pair of Youse. (*Pause.*) Jesus Christ you guys are out to fuckin lunch.

FRED. That's a bit rich coming from a convicted –

GIBB. Shut the fuck up Fred.

FRED. I'm sorry but I've taken enough insults tonight.

GIBB. So one more's no gonna hurt then is it?

MALONE'*s mobile rings.*

MALONE. Cheesy . . . No I'm still here. I'm leaving now. No I mean right now. Yea so make sure there's a drink waiting for me as soon as I walk in the door. A pint of lager and a double whisky, a good whisky, an make sure no cunt's sitting in my chair.

Pause.

GIBB. So what's the score?

MALONE. There is no score.

GIBB. What does that mean?

MALONE. It means you guys are on your own.

GIBB. What about the seven days?

FRED. Yea and you coming here out the goodness of your heart?

MALONE. I don't even know youse. If any cunt from the town wants to take you guys down that's their lookout. I shouldnae be getting involved in shite like this. I've got a wife and kids, you know that? I've got a chance to have a half-decent life, you know, nothing spectacular but . . .

GIBB. Half-decent.

MALONE. You get what I'm saying?

GIBB. I do.

MALONE. I'm too old for this. I've gotta move on. (*Pause.*) There's a bunch of guys in the pub and every fuckin one of them knows where I am, an if anything happened to your mate . . .

FRED. Gibby's just told you everything's cool.

MALONE. The point is if something did happen and police started asking questions, those same guys . . .

FRED. Who love you, respect you and fear you.

GIBB. D'you think they're all gonna lie for you?

MALONE. Put it this way, I wouldnae stick my mortgage on it.

FRED. No friends here ay?

Pause.

MALONE. Well boys I've got a drink waiting for me . . .

GIBB. So what d'you think's gonna happen?

MALONE. Hey you're asking the wrong guy. I'm officially retired. (*Pause.*) By the way was that really organic chicken?

FRED. Yea, it was.

MALONE. Taste the difference ay? Best of luck boys. (*Exits.*)

Pause.

FRED. So . . .

GIBB. What?

FRED. Fucked up night ay?

GIBB. A bit too fucked up.

FRED. Never easy is it?

GIBB. No . . . but it should be easier.

FRED. So what d'you think?

GIBB. I dunno, I'm thinking about it.

FRED. We should tidy the place up ay.

GIBB. Aye, I suppose it cannae hurt.

FRED *and* GIBB *start clearing up the mess.*

FRED. I don't mind doing the dishes if you clear the shit from the tables.

GIBB. Whatever.

FRED. In fact, Gibby.

GIBB. What?

FRED. Mibbe you should get Stewart's duvet . . . so he isnae cold when he wakes up.

GIBB. Aye okay.

FRED. Gibby.

GIBB. What?

FRED. Are you all right?

GIBB. I'm just tired. Heavy day you know.

FRED. Just get the duvet, I'll tidy everything up.

GIBB. All right then.

> GIBB *exits.* FRED *collects the plates and glasses and takes them to the sink.* GIBB *enters with the duvet and a pillow. Places the pillow under* STEW'*s head, covers* STEW *with the duvet and tucks him in.*

> See you in the morning.

FRED. Aye.

GIBB. We'll sort all this shit out.

FRED. Aye one way or another.

GIBB. Aye . . . Night then.

FRED. Hey Gibby.

GIBB. What?

FRED. Are you glad to be back? What's so funny?

GIBB. Nothing.

FRED. So . . . are you glad you came back?

GIBB. Course I am.

FRED. Least you know where you are ay.

GIBB. Night-night Fred. (*Exits.*)

FRED. Night-night Tone.

> FRED *gets a notepad from the kitchen drawer. Begins to write as he hums the tune to Hymn 412 – 'Will Your Anchor Hold'. He stops, tears up the page, starts on a fresh page, writes, stops, tears up the page and puts both pages in his pocket.*

> Fuck it.

> *Gets on with cleaning up the mess, singing as the lights fade:*

> Will your anchor hold in the storm of life
> When the clouds unfold their wings of strife?

When the strong tides lift, and the cables strain
Will your anchor drift, or firm remain?
We have an anchor that keeps the soul
Steadfast and sure while the billows roll
Fastened to the rock which cannot move
Grounded firm and deep in the Saviour's love.

Blackout.

Scene Five

Early morning. Still dark outside. The debris from the night before has gone. STEW *lies asleep on the sofa. A brick comes flying through the living-room window.*

STEW *wakes suddenly. He peers out the window from behind the curtains, then goes to the hallway. The curtains flap as the cold air fills the room.*

STEW. Gibby . . . Fred. (*Pause.*) Gibby . . . Fred. (*Exits.*)

GIBB (*offstage*). What is it?

STEW (*offstage*). Just come down.

GIBB (*offstage*). What time is it?

STEW (*offstage*). I dunno, just come down.

STEW *enters. Gets the brick.*

GIBB *enters wearing boxer shorts and T-shirt.*

GIBB. What's up? Fuck me it's cold in here. (*Wraps himself in the duvet.*)

STEW. Check it out.

GIBB. It's a fuckin brick.

STEW. Yea, I know.

GIBB. Why have you got it?

STEW. Cos it just came through the window.

GIBB. Oh . . .

STEW. Yea . . .

GIBB. Fuck.

STEW. That's what I was thinking.

GIBB. I better wake up ay. (*Looks out of window.*) There's nobody there. Is the back door locked?

STEW (*checks the back door*). Yea it's locked.

GIBB. Right, I'm on the case. First things first, I'll wake Fred up, you stick the kettle on.

STEW. Tea or coffee?

GIBB. Coffee. (*Exits.*)

STEW *puts the kettle on. Takes a couple of paracetamol, charges his mobile phone then continues making the coffee.*

GIBB *enters, fully dressed.*

Better make that just two cups.

STEW. Fred no wanting any?

GIBB. Fred's fuckin gone. He's not in his bed anyway.

STEW. I don't fuckin believe this. (*Gets the time from his mobile.*) It's six in the morning, where the fuck's he gonna be this early?

GIBB. I dunno.

STEW. Wait a minute . . . his car.

GIBB (*sticks his head out of the living room window*). It's gone.

STEW. I'm sorry but I'm totally lost, you know. I just got woken up by a low-flying brick, my best mate's fucked off, I've got a bandage wrapped round my head and I seem to be suffering from a mild case of amnesia. Two sugars you take ay?

GIBB. No just the one.

STEW. You best tell me what the fuck's goin on cos the last thing I remember is drinking whisky and having a sing-song.

GIBB. Malone came round last night. He said we had seven days to get the fuck out of town or all hell would break loose.

STEW. Where the fuck was I when this was happening?

GIBB. You were passed out on the sofa due to a combination of drink, drugs and Fred hitting you with the wok.

STEW. Fred hit me?

GIBB. You wouldnae eat his stir-fry and he took it a bit to heart. So he hit you, hence the bandage.

STEW. Did he mean to hit me?

GIBB. Oh aye I would say he definitely meant to hit you.

STEW. He takes his cooking quite seriously.

GIBB. So it seems, even so I think the bastard over-reacted.

STEW. Fuckin sounds like it to me.

GIBB. But . . . I think there's a bit more to it than that.

STEW. More than what?

GIBB. More than Fred throwing a wobbler purely on the grounds
that you were too fucked out your face to take on a plate of stir-
fry, you get what I'm sayin? I think it's been building up.
Anyway he knocked you out and then he started going on about
the Martians and if they landed on earth.

STEW. What's all that about?

GIBB. You don't want to know. Anyway, then Malone showed up.

STEW. And Malone said we had seven days to get the fuck out –

GIBB. That's what he said at first. He said he'd make sure we
wouldnae get any bother from the natives then it all went pear-
shaped and he kinda went back on that. He doesnae want to get
involved, in case he goes back inside. And basically that's you
up to date.

STEW. But what about Fred?

GIBB. I'm just as much in the dark about Fred as you are.

STEW. Here's your coffee.

GIBB. Cheers.

STEW. So what was it like?

GIBB. What was what like?

STEW. His stir-fry, did you have any?

GIBB. I had a small portion.

STEW. You wernae hungry either?

GIBB. No, but I ate what I could.

STEW. So what did you think?

GIBB. Well as chicken stir-fries go it was one of the best I've
tasted but what the fuck has that got to do with anything?

STEW. I don't fuckin know, my head's still up my arse.

Pause.

GIBB. I think the brick's just a warning. I think this means basically it's time to move on, time to get the fuck out of dodge you know.

STEW. Well I've no objections to that.

GIBB. Good, then all we need to do is make sure we don't get more of this kind of crap.

STEW. How are we gonna do that?

GIBB. I dunno, maybe the three of us take a walk down the street, with our heads held high and tell everyone that they got what they wanted and that we're leaving. If anyone gives us hassle we say we're sorry, we never meant any harm and we don't think we're better than anyone. As long as nobody gets violent I reckon that should be enough.

STEW. And if it isn't?

GIBB. We do what we have to do to pacify the situation, I dunno, we make like we're from the United Nations and we're here to keep the peace.

STEW. Who cares ay? We just take the money and get the fuck out.

GIBB. Better get a hold of Fred then ay?

STEW. Maybe you should call him. I don't feel up to it.

GIBB *dials.*

What's up, no answer?

GIBB. Nah, his phone's switched off.

STEW. That sucks.

GIBB. Seems a bit odd to me.

STEW. I feel like my head's gonna cave in.

Pause.

I don't fuckin believe it.

GIBB. What?

STEW. He's gone.

GIBB. What he's *gone* gone?

STEW. Aye . . .

GIBB. You sure?

STEW. Aye I'm sure . . . Fuckin bastard.

GIBB. Eh . . . d'you want to share this with me Stew?

STEW. D'you see what's missing?

GIBB. Well he's gone, his car's gone, I never really checked his room.

STEW. No, in the room, this room.

GIBB. Something's missing?

STEW. Aye . . . what a cunt.

GIBB. I'm baffled, sorry, I give up.

STEW. The cookery books, the ones that took up half that shelf.

GIBB. Oh aye . . . Fuck.

STEW. The cunt's fucked off, I'm telling you. You can check his room if you like, but if the books are gone . . .

GIBB. That's a bit fuckin rude ay?

STEW. I think he cared more about his fuckin cookery books than he cared about me.

GIBB. I'll check his room. (*Exits.*)

STEW *looks for his cigarettes, finds them, lights up.*

GIBB *enters.*

He's taken his fuckin clothes, cleaned out his cupboards an everything. (*Pause.*) Even taken the posters off the wall.

Pause.

STEW. Wait a minute.

GIBB. What?

STEW *exits out of kitchen door.*

STEW (*offstage*). I'll fuckin kill him. I swear to God I'll fuckin kill him. You're no gonna believe this.

GIBB. Believe what?

STEW *enters carrying a large cutting of rhubarb that's been pulled up by the roots.*

STEW. The bastard's ran off wi the stash.

GIBB. What stash?

STEW. The stash we kept under the rhubarb.

GIBB. I thought . . . Fred told me you kept everything at Celia's.

STEW. Naw man, we used to keep the Charlie at Celia's. The money . . . Jesus man there was over ten grand in there. (*Takes a couple of Valium.*) What a fuckin . . . I worked my fuckin bollocks off for that money.

GIBB. I don't know what to say mate.

STEW. Tell me something, do I have cunt written across my forehead?

GIBB. No.

STEW. Well at least that's something. (*Puts his jacket on, checks for his car keys.*) Are you coming?

GIBB. Where?

STEW. I'm gonna find the cunt and break his fuckin neck.

GIBB. Where you gonna go?

STEW. London.

GIBB. London? Are you daft?

STEW. He was always talking about this catering school in Mayfair. Maybe he's . . . I dunno I think he felt I was holding him back. (*Pause.*) Are you gonna come with me?

GIBB. I think I better stay here . . . just in case. (*Pause.*) I'll find something to fix the window up, cos this draught's a fuckin killer.

STEW. Aye. (*Pause.*) See you. (*Gives* GIBB *a hug.*) You're my best fuckin mate ay?

GIBB. Yea, course I am.

STEW. Laters then.

GIBB. Aye laters man. Oh by the way Stew.

STEW. What?

GIBB. There's a couple of things I need to tell you . . . when you get back like.

STEW. Right.

GIBB. Aye, you know . . . nothing major.

STEW. Well . . . I'll see you when I get back then.

GIBB. Aye, take care.

STEW *exits. Pause.*

GIBB. Cunt . . . nah no you me . . . guys I cannae tell you how good it is to be back. To breathe in the fresh air, look out the window an see the cows in the field. London kinda sucks guys it really does. You don't know where the fuck you are, who's who or what's what half the time. (*Pause.*) So, ma reasons, for goin? What can I say, the walls were coming in and I needed to be somewhere else . . . but I want to tell you why I came back. (*Pause.*) It was like I had an epiphany, you know what one of those is don't you? Good . . . See, I met this guy in a pub in Holloway, he was from Fife . . . Kingskettle of all places. We got talking and he was telling me about how he'd just split up with his bird and he was all broken-hearted. He had this bird who was about thirty-five and though she wasnae exactly fat you could say that physically her best years were past her. But this guy didnae mind at all cos the way he saw it is that fat birds, they're happy to have you. They go the extra yard, you know, they're more permissive and they let you try things out. See now this guy's thing was arse-licking . . . he fuckin loved to lick arse, couldnae get enough of it. So he's got this lassie an he's working on his arse technique, I mean those were his exact words, he wanted to work on his arse technique. So about three months of this go by, you know, him going out with this girl and all he does is licks her arse and he's getting really good at it and she likes it but at the same time she's wondering why he never shags her. So she gives him the ultimatum. There's gonna be no more arse-licking unless he shags her. I mean that's it, she's no gonna budge, it's shag me or find someone else. So what does he do? He gives her the elbow, tells her where to sling it, and now the cunt's in tatters . . . So I'm listening to the story an I keep picturing this guy going down and getting in about this big girl's arse and to be honest I just don't know how I feel about it cos there's this one thought sticking in my mind. So I ask him. Was her arse clean? An he says . . . oh aye her arse was clean . . . mine's wasnae, but hers was. I fuckin hosed myself . . . this mad Fifer an his stupid arse-licking story. I dunno I was a bit down but he made me laugh again . . . Two weeks later I was on the train.

Enter STEW. *Throws his car keys on the table. Slumps down on the sofa.*

That was quick.

STEW (*mumbling slightly*). There's no petrol in the car.

GIBB What was that?

STEW (*snapping*). There's No Fuckin Petrol In The Car.

Blackout.

End.

A Nick Hern Book

East Coast Chicken Supper first published in Great Britain
as a paperback original in 2005 by Nick Hern Books Limited,
14 Larden Road, London W3 7ST in association with
the Traverse Theatre, Edinburgh

Cover image: Euan Myles

Typeset by Country Setting, Kingsdown, Kent CT14 8ES
Printed and bound in Great Britain by Bookmarque, Croydon,
Surrey

A CIP catalogue record for this book is available from
the British Library

ISBN-13   978 1 85459 892 9
ISBN-10   1 85459 892 9